DO YOU RECOGNIZE THIS SABOTEUR?

PERSONALITY TRAITS: Cunning, sneaky, secretive, convincing, and persistent. A fast learner who takes positive ideas and principles and gives them a self-defeating, self-destructive twist.

METHODS OF OPERATION: Cynical, fearful, critical, pushy, worrying thoughts that undermine your self-confidence.

ENERGY SOURCE: Feelings of loneliness, fear, hurt, and anger that arise in response to "Don't be" and "Don't be who you are" messages.

DISGUISES: May sound supportive of your goals, but does so with criticism, "I shoulds," and "I musts" that actually encourage you to revel and undermine yourself. May put a smile on your face when you are really feeling sad or upset, urge you to say "yes" or "no" when you feel the opposite, or give a cackling, raucous laugh about something that is not funny.

➢ ➢ ➢

FIND OUT HOW THE SABOTEUR GOT INTO YOUR LIFE...WHAT IT DOES TO YOU DAILY...AND HOW TO CHANGE ITS POWER FROM DESTRUCTION TO A POSITIVE FORCE FOR FULFILLING THE BEST YOU CAN BE!

SELF-SABOTAGE

HOW TO STOP IT & SOAR TO SUCCESS

MARTHA BALDWIN, M.S.S.W.

(formerly published as
NURTURE YOURSELF TO SUCCESS)

A Time Warner Company

I have changed identifying details and created composites in the examples I have used throughout this book.

Martha Baldwin

Warner Books Edition

This Warner Books edition is published by arrangement with Rainbow Books, 2299 Riverside Drive, P.O. Box 1069, Moore Haven, FL 33471.

Warner Books, Inc., 1271 Avenue of the Americas, New York, NY 10020

Visit our Web site at http://warnerbooks.com

Printed in the United States of America
First Warner Books Printing: May 1990
20 19 18 17 16 15 14 13 12

Library of Congress Cataloging-in-Publication Data
Baldwin, Martha, 1941–
[Nurture yourself to success]
Self-sabotage : how to stop it and soar to success / by Martha Baldwin. — Warner Books ed.
p. cm.
Reprint. Originally published: Nurture yourself to success. Moore Haven, FL : Rainbow Books, ©1987.
Includes bibliographical references (p.).
ISBN 0-446-39108-5
1. Success—Psychological aspects. 2. Self-defeating behavior. 3. Nurturing behavior. I. Title.
BF637.S8B325 1990 89-70605
158'.1—dc20 CIP

Dedication

To all my teachers and especially my daughters, Lucie and Leigh, who opened my heart with their love, integrity, and courage.

Acknowledgment

My thanks to all my friends and professional associates who have encouraged and helped me create this book: and especially, Peggy Bryant, Sandy Morrison, Michelle Goodwin, Joan Bolmer, Erik Dalton, Anne Southern, Barbara and Jim Allen, Bill Brown, Richard Fiske, Carolyn Conger, Brugh Joy, Jerry Fankhauser, Jut and Elissa Meininger, Joyce Ingram, Gary Baldwin, Katherine Wise, Joe LaRocca, Liz Holt, Debi Pettigrew, Marilyn Ratzlaff and Betty Wright.

CONTENTS

FOREWORD

Robin Norwood, in her best-selling book, identified fifteen patterns that are common in the lives of *WOMEN WHO LOVE TOO MUCH*. She touched a cord deep in the hearts of women who found their lives reflected in her words. Support groups for Women Who Love Too Much have developed throughout the United States.

Men have found these patterns prevalent in their lives, too. For the truth is, we are a culture that loves too much and loves in destructive ways.

To stop "loving too much" we must learn to love without hurting ourselves or others. Once we master the art, loving too much is no longer an issue. It is impossible to love others too much when we are skilled in both the being and the doing of love. Instead we love ourselves and others responsibly, freely, with respect, and with humility and gratitude. With this understanding and practice of love, there cannot be too much.

Love is a skill; a skill we must seek and master. When we love too much, we aren't really loving at all. Instead we are being overly protective, ignoring limits and boundaries that separate one person's life and responsibilities from another's, and failing to take responsibility for nurturing ourselves adequately.

Love is real; it is the one reality we can absolutely count on and absolutely trust. Love can hurt and love can heal.

We can use it either way. Love that heals is freely expressed with responsibility and commitment, caring and giving, respect and intimacy, humility and a deep knowing of self and other. Giving and receiving love are essential to health, well-being, joy, and success.

When we experience loving unconditionally, we have developed a deep level of self-awareness, acceptance of our worth as spiritual beings, self-esteem based upon how we are creating our lives, self-love that embraces all of who we are, self-confidence that recognizes our capacities to cope with whatever challenges life presents, and self-respect that acknowledges and respects the validity and integrity of our emotions and our life experiences. The sum of all these components goes beyond them to ignite self-realization and the state of being that is unconditional love. (For a beautiful exploration and explanation of these concepts, see the video tape by Lazaris titled *UNCONDITIONAL LOVE* and published by Concept Synergy, P. O. Box 159 (M), Fairfax, CA 94930. 415-456-4855. 1985)

NURTURE YOURSELF TO SUCCESS is about learning to love responsibly. It shows you how to stop loving others too much while also ending self-sabotage. It teaches you to center yourself in the energy of love and embrace all the partial selves within you. It respects the boundaries that define you and encourages you to maintain the integrity of those boundaries so your relationships are healthy and satisfying.

As you learn to love responsibly and skillfully, others will catch the energy of your personal growth and self-realization. Imagine the possibilities as skillful loving becomes the norm on the planet we share. Our blessings will multiply exponentially as each of us takes full responsibility for the miracle of the life and the world we create.

INTRODUCTION

For the past eleven years I have worked as a psychotherapist teaching hundreds of people to nurture themselves adequately and lovingly. Early in my experience as a therapist, I realized that as adults all of us are responsible for growing up, completing our parenting process and correcting any destructive parenting we experienced as children. To meet these challenges we must take responsibility for learning what constitutes healthy nurturing. The goal is to develop a truly nurturing and unconditionally loving internal parent for the child that lives within us and is the essence of who we are.

The capacity to nurture ourselves includes knowing how to center our minds and hearts in the energy of love. It involves cultivating a loving aware consciousness of all of our internal selves, and especially the Inner Child and the fearmonger part I call the Saboteur. Self-nurturing also requires recognizing and accepting the physical, emotional, and mental boundaries that define and separate one person from another. This enables us to set loving limits for ourselves and with other people.

As a culture we have lost sight of the importance of knowing how to adequately nurture ourselves and live in loving relationships with others. We fail to respect the boundaries that separate one life from another and neglect setting loving limits with ourselves and with others. We love others too much and neglect our responsibility for nurturing ourselves.

And we suffer from the problems that arise when these processes are ignored. Patterns of addiction and co-dependence, disintegrating relationships; enmeshed, dysfunctional families; irresponsible, rebellious young people; sexual promiscuity and confusion; financial woes; degenerating health; and impaired self-expression all reflect our deficits in understanding and practicing truly nurturing attitudes and behavior.

Much is written about overcoming limitations and tapping into our vast untapped potential for creativity and abundant living. The paradox is that one of the major limitations we have to overcome is created by our lack of understanding of the function and importance of healthy nurturing, including accepting individual limits and the boundaries that exist between human beings.

In the ultimate sense, we are all connected and a part of The Source of the Life and Energy of the Universe, the Love of God. Yet in this dimension of time and space in which we meet, we are also individuals charged with the responsibility of our own lives and the challenge of fulfilling our life purpose.

To claim that responsibility and face our challenge, we must know how to find our center and ground ourselves in God's love. Within that center which is a reservoir of strength and innate wisdom, there is balance and the capacity to take charge of our lives. Here we realize that in the deepest sense of "what is" about life, everyone else has this capacity to take charge of his own being too. We are released from the illusion of being our brother's keeper rather than our own.

As we honor our own lives and resources, we release the people we love to responsibility for their lives and the choices they make. There is no need to continue trying to control other people. We know this is impossible. Instead, we take hold of controlling what we can be in charge of which is ourselves. What a relief! What a challenge!

We release ourselves from the traps we created clinging to others and sabotaging ourselves out of fear of growing up and letting go of our props. Now we are free to claim the abundant wealth, health, happy relationships and free self-expression that are our birthright. Life is simple rather than complex. We are free to love ourselves and others without guilt and self-pity. We claim the truth about ourselves, knowing that we are truly the creators of our own reality.

Low self-esteem is a relic of the past! As we grow up and claim the fullness of our power and resources, we feel wonderful about ourselves and about life. We are a microcosm of the universe, gods of our minds, emotions and bodies. And we are individual cells in the body of God, part of the ultimate creative force of the universe.

Through centering, knowing all of who we are, and keeping our boundaries intact, we move beyond limitation and self-sabotage into the full focused power we possess to live in prosperity and abundance. The choice is ours, moment by moment, throughout our lives. And when we encounter physical death, the ultimate limit of life in this dimension, we are free to move beyond this material plane knowing we made full use of the gift of a lifetime.

Martha Baldwin

CHAPTER I

NURTURING YOUR INNER CHILD

Growing up means taking full responsibility for loving and successfully nurturing the Inner Child that lives deep within you. No matter how well or how poorly the parenting people in your life did their jobs, the challenge of nurturing yourself successfully is yours once you grow beyond childhood and adolescence.

Instead of growing up and taking responsibility for your nurturing, you may have sought instead to nurture others, hoping that they will reciprocate by tending to your needs and feelings. This model, which both women and men in our culture are scripted to follow, creates painful, guilt ridden, disappointing relationships. It serves to keep us stuck and frustrated, loving others too much, while neglecting ourselves. Resentfully, but valiantly, we may keep on martyring ourselves, trying to control other people's lives, while refusing to take charge of our own. Exhausting ourselves in efforts to control what we cannot control, we abuse ourselves and ignore our responsibility to ourselves which we can control.

If this pattern is uncomfortably familiar to you, you probably are following the example your parents set for you and taught you to value. Your model for nurturing yourself is based on your experience with your parents. If theirs was a healthy, effective pattern of loving, nurturing, and limit setting, you have a strong base to build upon.

But, if your parents, using the models they absorbed from their parents, were not as effective in their relationship with each other and in their parenting of you as you needed them to be, you face the challenge of teaching yourself as an adult to nurture yourself successfully.

Nurturing yourself successfully means loving, acknowledging, and accepting the Inner Child that is the essence of who you are. It also means focusing and centering the power of your mind in the energy of love so you think clearly, positively, and constructively. When you develop a truly loving, nurturing parent for yourself, allied with a healthy, positively focused mind, your Inner Child will thrive in the internal climate of unconditional love and acceptance you create moment by moment for yourself. Moreover, your internal world of love and positive energy will be reflected in your outer world in loving, productive relationships with others. As you know and experience that you can take care of yourself adequately and happily, you won't be tempted into loving others too much while they neglect their responsibilities for themselves and their commitments to you.

Your external relationships mirror the quality of your relationship with yourself. If you are having difficulty in your relationships with others, you can allow those relationships to teach you about what is happening inside you among the various parts of yourself. Chances are you are acting out those inner relationships in your behavior patterns with other people.

Other people need to express themselves honestly and be loved, acknowledged, and accepted by you. They need to know you will be honest with them and say no to them when no is what you feel. They need to know you will say how you feel and what you need and release them to respond honestly, whatever their response may be. And you need to know they will reciprocate, honestly telling you what they need and feel, and releasing you to respond in the way that fits for you.

In a similar way, your Inner Child needs to know it is loved, acknowledged and accepted unconditionally by you. It wants to be listened to, honored, and parented effectively. It is most comfortable when it can trust you to give it protection by thinking clearly and lovingly, and saying no to the fearful, critical thinking, self-sabotaging parts of you. It needs to know you will say no to others when that is necessary to honor your child's legitimate needs and feelings. Your Inner Child also needs to trust that you will say no to it when its demands are excessive, when it thinks it has to have exactly what it wants immediately, and when it tries to con you into doing what is not in your best interests.

It is helpful to picture the little girl or little boy within you. You may want to find pictures of yourself as a child. You can have ones that you particularly like enlarged and put them in places where you will see them frequently and be reminded to remember your Inner Child in the present. Probably you will be most attracted to pictures of yourself when you were happy and obviously enjoying life. Seeing the Happy Child clearly is important. Cherish these pictures and keep them close to your heart.

You may find it harder to remember and let yourself see the other side of the child within you. The hurt, frightened, angry, abused, sad, isolated child is much more difficult to love, acknowledge, listen to, and accept. Yet this is the child within you that most needs to be seen, faced, loved, and through love and acceptance, healed of its pain and distress.

You may be accustomed to hiding the little girl or little boy inside you that is crying, hurting, bruised, bloody, or even beaten. It is hard to look at a child with a runny nose, a depressed face, and eyes that mirror pain and hurt. You may want to conceal this child and not let yourself or anyone else see the depth of its despair. You may have turned your back on this part of yourself years ago and doubt that such a child has any place in your life.

But chances are that a hurt child does live deep within you. Some people have experienced much more abuse and hurt than others, but no one grows to adulthood without some difficult times, hurtful experiences, and periods of disappointment and loss.

If your parents helped you learn to express yourself in healthy ways when difficult, disappointing experiences rocked your world, you probably are carrying little pain from the past forward into the present and future. Unfortunately, this has not been our cultural norm, given the fear and denial of feelings that have existed for years. It is more likely that you learned to hide and then ignore the hurt child within you while being overly sensitive to that same hurt child part in others. If so, one of your challenges as an adult is to face your own Hurt Inner Child instead of neglecting it while trying to heal its counterpart in others. Once you find the courage to turn within and look at this part of you in a nurturing attitude of love and acceptance, you are on the way to healing yourself and making yourself and your relationships whole and healthy.

But, in order to see your Hurt Inner Child, you will have to look behind the walls you have erected to hide this painful part of yourself. There are many ways to conceal the hurt child within you. Perhaps you will recognize some of these patterns in your repertoire for disguising Your Hurt Inner Child. Do you hide your hurt child;

1. Behind a tough guy, macho facade?
2. Behind a superwoman, invulnerable exterior?
3. Behind an angry, blaming stance with others?
4. Behind compulsive behavior like overeating, alcohol and drug abuse, sexual promiscuity, overworking, or stealing from others?
5. Behind phobias?
6. Behind rescuing other people and trying to control

their lives?

7. Behind confusion and helplessness?
8. Behind irrelevant behavior?
9. Behind super-reasonable, controlling behavior?
10. Behind self-destructive, suicidal behavior?

You may be fooling only yourself if you are stuck in some of these patterns. Other people probably recognize your pain or at least see your behavior as the distortion that it is. The tragedy is that until you can see and be your real self, you consistently will alienate yourself from other people who love you and could support you as you work your way out of your pain.

When you are ready to go beyond your defensive walls to face and acknowledge your Hurt Inner Child, you must begin the process of developing a loving relationship with this shy, frightened part of yourself. Gaining its trust will take time and patience. After all, you have ignored it for years and the child within you may take some convincing that you are serious in your intention to honor its existence, its needs, and its feelings now. This stage calls for consistent effort on your part to tune into Your Inner Child, to imagine that you are holding this child close to your heart and embracing it in love and light.

Once your Inner Child begins to feel safe with you and to trust that you really are interested in its existence, it will begin to share with you what you may have forgotten and neglected to notice for years. You may experience deep feelings of anger, hurt, sadness, loneliness, despair or helplessness. If you are willing to allow your Inner Child to share these feelings with you, and if you are able to nurture yourself through these experiences of self-revelation, you will find yourself growing stronger and more whole with every step you take in this process of ever-deepening self-acceptance and healing.

The key is keeping yourself centered in the energy of unconditional love while managing to protect your Inner

Child from other parts within you that may be intent upon sabotaging your progress. We will explore centering in unconditional love, the foundation for nurturing yourself to success, in the central sections of this book. We also will learn about other parts within you and how to set limits within yourself and keep your boundaries with others. But first, let's meet the Internal Saboteur, the part within you that is dedicated to defeating you in your efforts to nurture yourself successfully and claim the wholeness and healing you desire and deserve.

CHAPTER II

THE SABOTEUR AND ITS UNDERCOVER MISSION

For years I sabotaged myself and kept myself from having what I truly wanted in my life. Though I was successful in many ways during those same years, my successes were in providing services and help for other people and attaining high levels of academic achievement. The common denominator in those successes was pleasing other people; clients, friends, teachers, the world at large. On the side of my life that involved loving, pleasing, and satisfying myself, I made lots of costly mistakes.

Pleasing other people was congruent with the direct, verbal messages I received from both my parents as I grew up. I knew with absolute clarity that I existed to make other people happy. As long as I was reacting to what others wanted from me, I knew how to be successful and stay within the bounds of the messages my parents conveyed to me about how I should be in the world.

Whenever I came close to finding genuine happiness and personal satisfaction, I managed to sabotage myself. Again I stayed within the bounds of my parents' injunctions. For I knew deep inside myself that my own happiness, feelings, needs, and personal satisfaction didn't count. This message was communicated to me in indirect ways. It came not so much in words, as by implication and through direct experience. The implied message was "You're an object for someone else's use and pleasure.

How this hurts you is beside the point." I was told that my parents sacrificed everything for me. The implication was that I owed my life to them and to other people. All of this created tremendous confusion for me about what the boundaries were that separated my life from theirs.

The parenting messages I absorbed from my parents, I, in turn, used to parent myself. The parenting patterns I thus created for myself reflected both the negative, child-like, destructive aspects of my parents and the healthy, loving sides of them as well. From the healthy, loving parts of them, I learned that I was smart and possibly talented, that I was pleasing when I worked really hard, that hard work is possible and pays off, that life is fun sometimes (on vacations and special occasions), and that the spiritual dimension of life is really important. From their destructive, infantile parts I learned that I had no right to exist, that I could, at best, only hope to justify my existence by serving others and denying myself.

Thus equipped, I set out to live my life, armed with an excellent education with high academic honors, and psychological problems so deep it took me twenty years to uncover and resolve them. In the process I learned a lot about how to nurture and love myself in healthy ways. I also learned to stop the Saboteur within me.

The Saboteur is the energy pattern within us that follows the dictates of the "witch parent", that destructive, infantile parent part we incorporate in ourselves from the destructive, infantile, neurotic child parts of our parents. The "witch parent" or Saboteur inside us operates in powerful ways to direct our lives and destroy us in the process.

The Saboteur reflects the fearful, angry, selfish, destructive child within our parents that didn't want to be displaced by an external child that was helpless, demanding, and totally dependent. This fearful, jealous, angry child in our parents is a lot like a two-year-old who doesn't hesitate to say he'd like to flush the new baby down the toilet. He's been displaced. He isn't the only baby, the center of his parents' world any longer. In a similar way, the neurotic child part in our parents feels displaced by the new baby and is angry about it. Unless parents have some awareness of these feelings of rage and resentment, and through that awareness, some charge over how they're expressed, they will drive these ugly energies underground within themselves. Forced out of awareness, these dark feelings find expression in hidden, unconscious ways that are lethal to their children.

The rage of the destructive, displaced and disowned child in a parent is terrifying to her external child. Even though the parent may do her best to hide these frightening feelings, her baby is tuned into her through the deep mental, emotional, and psychic bond which exists between mother and child (and father and child). The child senses and experiences kinesthetically the feelings his parents have, even when parents may have no conscious awareness of these feelings themselves. And he gets the message they communicate in this subtle way.

This message is highly charged for the child because the feelings associated with it are so frightening. The child senses that he is not wanted, is not welcome in the world, and is not OK as he is. Even though his parents' verbal messages to him may be very loving and affirming, these contradictory, often nonverbal, subtle messages are powerful and lethal. At a deep, often completely unconscious level, the child gets that his parents are jealous of him, that they would rather not have him around. Because he may be preverbal and he is terrified of the rage he senses behind these messages, he is not free to express directly his fear, hurt, anger, sorrow, and feelings of isolation and abandonment. Instead he turns these feelings on himself. In effect, he decides to destroy or cripple himself in order to avoid his parents' anger and not upset the neurotic, destructive internal children in them. Better to feel some control over his own destruction than to be the helpless victim of their anger which seems deadly to him.

The Internal Saboteur evolves to carry out within the child's life the lethal messages he unconsciously absorbed from his parents. The Saboteur turns the child's hurt and anger about these messages against the child himself to avoid directing these feelings at his parents who are essential to his survival. The process of self-destruction and self-sabotage that is set in motion usually is long, slow, and subtle. It is a mystery to the child himself and to his parents. Why does he consistently manage to stop short of accomplishing what he is capable of achieving? Why does he become sick, depressed, and frail? Why does he get into drugs, alcohol, or sexual promiscuity when he knows how destructive these choices can be? Why does he pick friends who are troublemakers? Why does he sabotage himself just when he is close to reaching a goal?

The answers to these questions lie in the unconscious decisions he made early in life to avoid neurotic parental rage. He must not be more successful than his parents have been. He must not threaten them and arouse the angry monster in them. Instead he will do away with himself, directly or indirectly.

These early decisions will eventually be deadly unless he brings them into consciousness, expresses his long buried feelings of hurt, sorrow, anger, fear, and abandonment, and redecides about his right to live his own life in his own way. To do this he must grow up and claim the power he possesses to see clearly and accept all of himself, including his frightening feelings and his Internal Saboteur. Then he must learn to nurture himself lovingly and adequately, express himself honestly, and say "no" to the Internal Saboteur whenever it appears. Once he can see the Saboteur, feel its energy, hear its words, and express the fear, rage, hatred and sorrow that fuel its attacks on him, he is free to take charge of his life and have a choice about whether or not he allows the Saboteur to undermine him and dash his fondest dreams.

And you can stop sabotaging yourself when you identify your Internal Saboteur, know how it thinks, and feel how its energy operates in your life. In order to see the Saboteur clearly, you must look from the very center of your being. From this core, you can see and feel the myriad parts that operate within you. Some of these energy patterns you learned from others. Others you created to survive and protect yourself in the world. All these parts feel and think and sometimes even take you over and direct your life according to their wishes and desires.

The Saboteur is one of those parts. It also uses other parts for its destructive purposes. It usually is quite clever and cunning in its approach. It may flatter your vulnerable subselves, gaining their confidence and support, and then use them for its own destructive purposes. Like a skilled con artist, it knows its power, your weak points, and how to manipulate you into doing its bidding while ignoring your own better judgment.

Ignoring the Saboteur empowers it. Trying to get rid of it only teaches it to hide itself in more clever ways. The only route to ending self-sabotage is through facing and knowing the Saboteur intimately. Only then can you acknowledge its destructiveness, accept its presence, learn to contain its power, and say "no" to its attempts to destroy your life. It is only when you ignore and deny its existence that the Saboteur can do its deadly work secretly and successfully.

Ultimately when you can see and accept the Saboteur within you, express the feelings that energize it, and set limits with it effectively, it will be transformed. Just as an angry, destructive child is healed through loving acceptance and firm limits, the Saboteur, too, can be healed when it is acknowledged and dealt with appropriately. You don't get rid of it; you set your intention to heal it of its fearful destructive, angry attacks on your life. The goal is to redirect its brilliant, creative, persistent, and powerful energies to help you realize your own purposes for your life.

Nurturing yourself to success means squarely facing the Saboteur within you and gaining mastery over it. It is an exciting journey toward self-acceptance, full responsibility and personal empowerment. Embracing all of who you are, you can get where you want to go with all your resources available to support and enable you.

Even the Saboteur has its valuable side. It helps you find your strength, know your vulnerability, and discover the essence of your power and responsibility to be fully in charge of the way you direct your life.

CHAPTER III

THE SABOTEUR: A PROFILE

ENERGY SOURCE: Feelings of isolation, abandonment, fear, sorrow, hurt, and anger that arise in response to "Don't be" and "Don't be who you are" messages. These messages are communicated, frequently unconsciously and early in life, by disowned and destructive energy patterns in your parents.

MISSION: To do away with you so you won't threaten these neurotic, angry child parts of your parents. To do this in both subtle and not so subtle ways so you think it was your own idea in the first place.

METHODS OF OPERATION: Cynical, fearful, critical, pushy, worrying thoughts that undermine your self-confidence. Rebellious, negative suggestions that are calculated to defeat you and keep you from accomplishing your goals. Cunning, conning comments that are designed to confuse you and seduce you into going against your better judgment.

PERSONALITY TRAITS: Cunning, devious, clever, subversive, sneaky, secretive, conning, brilliant, convincing, and persistent. A fast learner who can take positive ideas and principles and give them a self-defeating, self-destructive twist. For example, "Let go and let God" becomes "Sit back and do nothing."

TACTICS: Uses stressful times to launch powerful attacks on your self-confidence, integrity, and commitment to yourself. Swings into action whenever you begin to be too successful or to enjoy being alive too much. Becomes very active when you begin to make positive changes in your life. Doesn't like therapists or books that blow its cover. Will redouble its efforts to control you when you begin to recognize its activity in your life. In order to do this, becomes even more clever and subtle.

DISGUISES AND CLUES: May sound as if it is supporting your goals, but does so in a critical, heavy-handed way that actually encourages you to rebel and undermine yourself. May put a smile on your face when you are actually feeling sad or upset; may nod your head in a "no" gesture when consciously you want to say "yes" or vice versa. May give a cackling, raucous laugh about something which is not funny.

CHAPTER IV

SEEING YOUR SABOTEUR

What destructive messages did you receive from your parents? Transactional Analysis describes the witch parent, which usually operates outside the conscious awareness of our parents, and delivers two kinds of injunctions. The most lethal category of messages boils down to "Don't exist", countered by a strong demand to "Be perfect". Less deadly, but also destructive, are parental injunctions that amount to "Don't be who you are", countered by "Be who and what we want you to be".

"Don't exist" injunctions may be delivered casually through statements like, "If I hadn't gotten pregnant with you, your father and I wouldn't have had to get married". Or "We didn't really want a third child. I almost got an abortion." "If it weren't for you I would have . . . " or "Your mother almost died when you were born. You tore up her body".

A child, hearing statements like these, gets the strong impression that he wasn't wanted and has done nothing but cause trouble. He feels rejected, guilty, and unloved. He may respond by trying to be perfect to justify his existence and make up to his parents for the hurt and trouble he believes he causes them. Or he may opt to be a real trouble-maker, engaging in blatantly self-destructive behavior unconsciously calculated to carry out his parents' "Don't exist" messages. Being either perfectly wonderful or perfectly terrible creates a prison of self-destruction and self-sabotage.

"Don't be who you are" messages invite a child to disown and reject vital aspects of his being. Specific injunctions in this category include "Don't feel or show emotion"; "Don't be the sex you are" (We really wanted a boy but we got you); "Don't think" (Let me think for you); "Don't" (Be very cautious, don't do anything); "Don't be close to other people" (Be my child forever).

The child who receives such messages may comply by trying to fit himself into the mold his parents cast for him. Who he really is doesn't count. He is supposed to be the person his parents want him to be. Or he may rebel, expressing an extreme version of the behavior his parents wanted to eliminate. For example, a woman with a strong "Don't feel" injunction may spend years in therapy, stuck in her emotions, and afraid to own her power to heal her life.

Since these destructive injunctions are unconsciously sent and unconsciously received, the child's decisions in response are unconscious too. Years later he will still be living out his early decisions unless he brings these destructive messages into clear conscious awareness and makes a new decision to live fully and be exactly who he is. Once a new decision is made, he faces the moment-by-moment challenge of saying no to habitual, fearful, self-sabotaging patterns of thinking, feeling, and behaving.

When you decide to bring your parents' injunctions to you into conscious awareness, (see the exercise at the end of this chapter) your first task is to recognize, accept, express, and release your feelings of anger, sadness, and despair in response to those destructive messages. You may want to write a letter to your parents (for yourself, not necessarily to send to them) giving full expression to your emotions. You also may choose to talk aloud with your parents as if they were present, telling them exactly how you feel about these issues. The presence of a therapist or good support group can be extremely helpful in this process because the child within you has lived in fear of these destructive parental energies for years and may be reluctant to face into these feelings without external support, permission and encouragement.

Along with expressing and releasing these powerful old feelings, you also will want to redecide about how you choose to live your life now and in the future. A new decision to live and be fully who you are is the crucial first step in stopping self-sabotage. Once you decide your life counts, that you deserve to live it fully and be the real person you are, you are ready to look carefully at the Saboteur part within you to see how it operates. Realizing that its purpose is to carry out the self-destructive injunctions you received from your parents, you will want to look closely at how it uses fear to create havoc and unhappiness in your life.

Create your own mental image of how your Saboteur looks. You might imagine a cartoon type character, your own version of how such a tricky, clever, underground character might appear. Draw him for yourself and give him a name. Let yourself enjoy the process.

Armed with this image of your Saboteur and clear about his intentions for your life, you are ready to face your challenger. Your goal is to uncover his subversive activities within your mind and to short circuit his impact on your emotions, your behavior, and your health.

Join me now as we explore processes that will teach you to recognize and accept him when he appears, outwit him, set limits with him, and ultimately transform his destructive energy and bring harmony and unified purpose to your life. Your goal is not to get rid of the Saboteur. It is to tame him and harness his energy and creativity so he becomes an ally rather than an enemy. This is accomplished by letting go of your parents and their destructive messages, redeciding about your own purposes and goals, and taking charge of your life away from the Saboteur. You must learn to stop self-sabotage moment by moment and step by step until the Saboteur is no longer a destructive force, but is instead, a partner in your progress toward your goals.

EXERCISE: UNCOVERING PARENTAL INJUNCTIONS

ASK YOURSELF THE FOLLOWING QUESTIONS. IT WILL BE HELPFUL TO WRITE OUT YOUR ANSWERS.

1. How long do you expect to live? (If you think you will die at a relatively early age, ask yourself how you got that idea?)

2. How do you think you will die? (If you think you will suffer through a terrible illness or die in a tragic accident, how did you get that idea?)

3. What is your fondest dream? Do you see yourself attaining that dream? If not, where did you get the idea that you can't have what you really want?

4. Who named you and what is the meaning behind your name? What have you decided about yourself because of your name? How do you feel about your name?

5. What are the stories that are told about your mother's pregnancy with you and your birth? What messages about your life did you get from these stories?

6. What stories are told about you as a child? What messages about you come through these stories?

7. What was your favorite childhood story or fairytale? How is the theme of this story reflected in your life?

8. What are some of your most vivid childhood memories? Go back to those experiences and feel how you felt then. What conclusions did you draw about yourself and your life from those experiences? What decisions did you make as a result of those experiences? Do you want to change any of those conclusions and decisions now?

9. What predictions did your parents make about your future? How did you feel about those predictions? What did you decide in response to those predictions?

10. How did your parents react to your successes, interests, and activities when you were a child? Did they encourage you to try new things and find your own interests? Were you expected to fulfill their unfulfilled expectations?

11. What were the rules in your family about expressing your feelings (especially anger and sadness)? How did you adapt to these expectations?

12. Were you encouraged to think for yourself? Did your parents have confidence in your ability to take care of yourself responsibly?

13. What were you taught about taking risks and trying out new possibilities? How did you respond?

14. Is it difficult for you to remember either the negative or the positive about your parents and your childhood experiences? What are you afraid of if you let yourself see the whole picture of your early experiences?

LIST THE PARENTAL MESSAGES YOU UNCOVER

POSITIVE, CONSTRUCTIVE MESSAGES

NEGATIVE, DESTRUCTIVE MESSAGES

WHAT DID YOU DECIDE IN RESPONSE TO THESE MESSAGES?

ENABLING DECISIONS

SELF-SABOTAGING DECISIONS

HOW DO YOU WANT TO CHANGE YOUR SELF-SABOTAGING DECISIONS NOW?

HOW DO YOU FEEL ABOUT WHAT YOU'VE UNCOVERED?

Write a letter to each of your parents expressing your feelings as honestly as possible. Don't attack your parents. Instead tell them what you feel and how the messages you received from them have affected you. You may or may not choose to share these letters with them.

Write a letter to your Inner Child. Express your understanding and compassion for this core part of yourself. Tell your Inner Child how you will nurture it lovingly now and in the future.

Imagine yourself holding your Inner Child close to you in a warm, loving embrace. Listen to whatever it wants to share with you. Allow it to write to you if it wishes to do so. Assure this child of your reliable, nurturing presence in its life. Gently bring your child inside yourself and keep it near your heart.

CHAPTER V

REPRESSED ANGER: THE TIGER IN YOUR SABOTEUR'S TANK

Anger is the powerful emotion that rises in the child within us when we don't like something that is happening in our lives. Anger alerts us that we need to express ourselves in some way because we feel hurt, our needs and wants are being ignored, our feelings discounted, or our boundaries violated. Like pain, anger signals us that something is wrong. It tells us we need to pay attention to what's happening in our relationships with others and either say yes to our own needs and feelings, values and beliefs, or no to someone else who may be intruding on our lives in a way that is harmful and uncomfortable for us.

Anger emerges when the child within us fights accepting "what is" in our lives. We're angry when we face death, loss, and separation from people we love and need. Anger fills us when other people don't turn out to be as we want them to be or do what we want them to do. We are angry when we give our power to other people and then end up feeling helpless, dependent, and victimized. We're angry when society, laws, rules, and structures interfere with our freedom to do, be, and experience whatever we choose. We're angry when we encounter limits and boundaries between ourselves and other people, and when we see qualities in others that we fear and fail to acknowledge in ourselves.

Problems with anger are pervasive in our culture

because we have not learned ourselves, nor taught our children, how to master this fiery emotion we all experience. Anger is as natural and human as arms and legs, fingers and toes; but we pretend we can ignore it and make it go away. In effect, we reject the child within us who feels this powerful emotion. What starts as self-rejection in the effort to ignore anger, ends in disrupted relationships, divorce, migraine headaches, ulcers, colitis, and cancer. We give the Saboteur a powerful weapon to use against us when we reject the Inner Child and stuff anger inside ourselves without learning appropriate ways to clarify it, express it, and release it. The Saboteur, when we allow it to operate outside our conscious awareness, uses repressed anger to destroy our dreams, undermine our relationships with others, and damage our physical health.

Repressed anger is expressed unconsciously by the Saboteur in ways we don't plan and direct; like being late, forgetting, losing things, withdrawing from relationships, being irritating to other people, whining, feeling depressed, overeating, closing down sexually, pouting, and refusing to communicate. When the Saboteur turns repressed anger inward, the physical body gets in on the act, creating body pain that reflects those hot, angry feelings stuffed inside us with no other outlet for expression and release. Eventually, these stuffed feelings stored up over the years, can destroy health and even life itself if we don't learn to stop the Saboteur and master the monster emotion so we make it work for, rather than against, us.

Repressed anger also fuels volcanic, angry explosions that erupt when some incident, small or large, pushes us beyond what we can contain and ignore and the Saboteur takes us over. Then we become the angry monster, determined to force others to pay attention to the needs and feelings we have been ignoring ourselves. We want to frighten them into changing or doing our bidding. In our righteous wrath and indignation, we project our problems onto others, blame them, and demand that they change so we can be happy. We are oblivious to the source of our pain which lies within ourselves. We fervently believe at that moment that they are the cause of all our woe.

After we exhaust our rage and survey the damage we have done to the people we attacked, we experience remorse and horror at the intensity and destructiveness of our feelings. At this point, we probably vow anew to hide and repress these monstrous feelings so we will never again be guilty of such an outburst. The Saboteur chuckles gleefully as we make another loop in this vicious circle of our own creation; repression, explosion, remorse, guilt, repression, explosion, remorse, guilt. Nothing is solved. Nothing changes. Our bodies and our relationships still suffer, despite our occasionally relieving the mounting pressure inside us with an angry tirade.

Learning to notice anger when we feel it is the first step in mastering anger and taking control of its expression away from the internal Saboteur. This sounds simple enough, but if you have spent years ignoring anger, you're skilled at repressing these feelings so quickly that you simply don't notice them at all.

One way to break this habit is to review each day's activities, asking yourself what you have experienced that might have aroused angry feelings. What specifically did you feel angry about? Your goal is to notice angry feelings without judgment or self-criticism. This too is challenging because you may have believed for years that anger is bad and you are bad for feeling it. (You can explore your personal beliefs about anger by doing the exercises at the end of this chapter.)

Yet it is important for your health and emotional well-being that you decide to accept all of who you are, including the child within you who feels anger frequently. When you stop judging and rejecting this part of yourself, you'll have more energy, be less likely to feel depressed, and you'll feel more powerful. You also will have many more choices about expressing yourself honestly and appropriately in all your relationships with others.

Remember that your intention is to learn to express anger effectively. Expressing anger in ineffective, destructive ways is just as much a problem as not expressing your anger at all.

When you acknowledge your anger (without rejecting yourself for feeling it), get clear on what you're angry about and then ask yourself how you might have expressed yourself when your feelings first occurred. Practice expressing yourself when you are alone and can explore these feelings without dumping them on someone else. Remember when you say how you feel, its important to make "I" statements like "I felt angry about . . . because . . ." This is far more effective and appropriate than attacking the other person in a critical, judgmental way.

You also can write letters you don't intend to send and give yourself a chance to get your feelings out of you and onto paper. You can then decide whether or not you want to talk directly with the person with whom you're angry.

Gradually, you will begin to recognize your anger when it first arises. Now you have the choice of expressing yourself directly in the situation at hand. Like a child learning to walk, you may be awkward and clumsy expressing yourself at this stage in your growth process. The challenge is to learn from each experience and profit from your mistakes. Your goal is to be responsible with your anger; responsible for recognizing and accepting the child within you that has these feelings and responsible for handling these feelings effectively. The objective is not to allow your angry child to take you over and dominate your life. Be aware, though, that the Saboteur would like to seduce you into stopping your learning process at this point.

As you continue to explore your anger, you may find that your feelings go much deeper than the present day experiences you are encountering. If your anger escalates easily, feeds on itself, and comes out too intense for the situation at hand, you are tapping into feelings from the past, feelings you have repressed for years. Ask yourself what the present situation may be mirroring from your past. Is your anger with your husband also a reflection of anger with your father from years ago when you encountered a similiar pattern of interaction with him? Does your boss irritate you in just the way your mother used to when she tried to control your behavior? Is your child triggering your rage with your parents when she fights with you about an issue similar to one you haven't addressed with them?

When you become aware of your past impinging on the present, allow yourself to express your old angry feelings. You can speak with your parent as if he were present. Give him a chair to occupy and address him directly. You can even take his place, play his part, and respond to yourself as you intuitively know he might respond if he were physically present now. Continue your encounter, playing both roles, until you feel yourself ready to release your anger and let go of this old situation with understanding and forgiveness.

If you don't like role playing, write him a letter and say what you need to say. Each time you exhaust your anger over a past experience, you will feel freer, lighter, and more alive. Depression lifts as you release burdens you have carried, buried and petrified inside yourself for years. What a relief!

As you continue your growth process, your anger will become more manageable, less intense. By releasing ancient rage, the present becomes more and more pleasant, peaceful, and fulfilling. You are overcoming your fear of the child within you who feels anger. It is no longer an emergency to be angry or to encounter someone else who is angry. Anger is simply an emotion to be accepted, acknowledged, and released.

Letting go of your anger, once you have acknowledged and expressed it, is essential to your happiness and well-being. However, this is a step you may find yourself resisting. Sometimes the idea of letting go is frightening if you imagine that you might lose something or lose control in the process. The truth is that letting go, like exhaling, is simply a cleansing process, necessary to your health and well-being. If you find yourself holding onto your anger, practice breathing fully and completely. Exhale as completely as possible, contracting your abdominal muscles, then notice as your lungs fill naturally and completely with fresh air. Exhale again, visualizing your lungs emptying completely.

Continue your breathing and imagine that you can see your angry feelings moving out of your body and being transformed into clear white light that surrounds you in love. Feel how clear and open you are. Embrace the child within you and prepare to move on. The past is past and now is now. Forgive and forget. Let it go. Remember that it's the Saboteur inside you that urges you to hang on to old resentments and treasure old rage. It wants you to keep these dead feelings alive to fuel its attacks on you and your relationships with others.

Anger is a powerful tool for learning about yourself. By accepting anger and learning from it, you become much clearer about who you are and what is really important to you. Your anger helps you know and respect yourself.

Frequently what angers you with others reflects something you fear and fail to acknowledge in yourself. The more you accept yourself without judging and rejecting your human, less-than-perfect parts, the less anger you will feel toward others when their imperfections show, too.

The way toward less anger in your life is not the path of denial and self-rejection. Facing and accepting this emotion heals you of your fears and frees you to learn what each experience of anger has to teach. Paradoxically, anger fades as we stop fighting "what is" (including anger) in ourselves and others and learn to accept in love all the challenges life creates.

EXERCISES

Make a list of times you felt angry today. This week. During the past month.

Ask yourself what specifically angered you in these situations. Clarify your feelings.

How did you express these feelings directly and indirectly?

What patterns do you notice in the ways you respond to and express anger?

CHAPTER VI

LESSONS ON ANGER: YOUR EDUCATION FOR PERSONAL POWER

Your education about anger began when you were a toddler. As soon as you were able to crawl and explore your big, fascinating world, you began to assert your individuality and separateness from your parents. In the process, you encountered lots of "nos and don'ts". Powerful angry feelings rose inside you when you were frustrated in your explorations. Probably you expressed yourself in no uncertain terms with loud, angry tears, a red face, and maybe even kicking, fighting arms and legs. Your parents were interfering with your freedom. The world no longer seemed to revolve around you, so that your wants and needs were fulfilled without question. You protested angrily.

How your parents reacted to your rage was crucial to your development. If they were friendly with their own anger and able to experience and express it appropriately, they were not alarmed when they saw your anger emerge. They acknowledged your feelings without fear and began the process of teaching you to handle these powerful feelings in appropriate, constructive ways. "I understand that you are angry. It's OK to be angry, but it's not OK to hit me when you're angry." "It's OK to be angry, but you may not disrupt dinner. I'm going to put you in your room where you'll be safe until you're finished being angry. You can hit your pillow if you want to."

Your parents' attitudes about anger are the key to what you learned about this emotion when you were a child. If you felt and sensed your parents' calm acceptance of your angry feelings, you gradually learned to accept them without fear too. Eventually you learned to handle these powerful feelings constructively.

But if your parents were afraid of anger in themselves, you felt and sensed their fear when you became angry. You learned to associate fear with the experience of anger.

If your parents expressed their fear by becoming angry too, escalating their feelings over yours in a threatening, overpowering way, you became frightened of anger. You taught yourself to hide your rage from your parents so you wouldn't upset them. If this pattern was not interrupted or changed, you didn't progress beyond this level of development to master your anger. Instead you became more and more adept at stuffing your feelings inside yourself. You probably had periodic temper tantrums when you became really overloaded with repressed feelings and something provoked your buried rage. But these episodes also set off your parents' fears and reinforced your learning that anger is a bad, destructive monster to be avoided no matter what the cost to you.

If your parents were fearful, helpless, and ineffective in their efforts to cope with your anger, you learned that you could manipulate them with your rage. If this was your experience, you discovered power in your anger in a way that was destructive for you. You learned that you could get your way by using your anger as a weapon to frighten your parents and get them to accommodate to what you wanted. You became inappropriately powerful, holding the threat of an angry outburst over your parents' heads. They in turn tried to keep you happy and appeased to avoid your rages.

Either way, you got stuck in your developmental process. Rather than learning to master your anger through facing your feelings and learning to handle them in constructive, appropriate ways, you learned instead to fear the anger monster and hide it, or to use it to frighten others into doing your bidding.

Your anger remained like an untrained family dog that is kept fenced in the backyard. The dog is too undisciplined to be an enjoyable playmate for family members. If he accidentally gets into the house, he races about in his unbounded excitement, jumping on people and creating chaos and confusion. As soon as he can be caught, he is banished again to his backyard domain. He remains a lonely beast, isolated and confined, away from the warmth and love of his master's touch, discipline, and teaching. Unless the family decides to train him, love him, and make him a part of their lives, he is doomed to being a monster, nuisance dog, a problem to everyone he encounters.

If you didn't begin to learn as a child to master your anger, you may have had some serious problems by the time your teenage years rolled around. Anger repressers who have periodic temper outbursts may turn to drugs and alcohol, sexual acting out, failure in school, compulsive perfectionistic behavior, overeating, overachieving, depression, or even suicide. Pouting, passive refusal to act, and physical symptoms like stomachaches, headaches, hyperactivity, and allergies are common. Anger abusers also may turn to illegal activities, seeking to discover where the limits of their power lie.

Your parents (and other parenting figures like teachers, coaches, other kids' parents, and radio and television) were your anger teachers. You progressed in your learning about anger as far as they had progressed in theirs, unless you have taken responsibility as an adult for reeducating yourself about this powerful, important emotion.

Mastering anger is a challenge you can meet no matter what age you are when you decide to grow beyond your fears and into the fullness of your personal power and potential for health, happiness, and success.

EXERCISE:

How did your father express anger? How about your mother?

What did you parents believe about anger?

What expressions were used in your family to describe anger and angry people? (e. g. Mad as a wet hen. Blowing your top. Mad as a hornet's nest. Seeing red.)

CHAPTER VII

ANGER AND INTIMACY

Expressing anger appropriately in intimate relationships is a special challenge. And it is essential to maintaining a healthy and growing relationship that nurtures both partners and their commitment to each other.

If something you do angers your mate, you want to know what happened so you will have a choice about recreating that same kind of situation again. If your mate's behavior angers you, you need to tell him honestly what you are feeling. Communicating openly in this way helps you nurture your relationship. It gives you both more choices.

When you know you have angered your mate, you can examine the situation to discover what you have to learn from it. Sometimes you will see a pattern of behavior in yourself that you need to recognize and correct. This helps you grow. Other times, you will see that your mate's anger reflects pain and immaturity in him that he needs to face. Perhaps you have said "no" to something he wants you to do. Perhaps you have commented on something he doesn't want to notice. In these situations, you both will learn if you have the courage to look at yourselves as honestly as you can.

Growth demands that you master anger and allow it to teach you about yourself and your mate. One of the most frequent precipitators of anger in an intimate relationship is the mirror effect. When you see your mate doing something you don't like, or fear, in yourself, you probably will react in anger, wanting to stamp out this behavior you don't like to notice. Your mate is your mirror, reflecting back to you parts of yourself you may like to pretend do not exist.

Encountering boundaries between people in relationships also stirs up angry feelings, especially if you fight accepting the importance and inevitablility of boundaries and limits between people. When your mate says "no" to something you want, the child within you may be as angry as a two-year-old who has been told he can't have cake before dinner. The Inner Child wants what he wants and may put up a fight to get it, especially if he has discovered that anger is a potent weapon. As you grow to realize that no matter how much you love each other, you still are two separate people whose needs, desires, and interests are not always identical, you develop the capacity to accept your differences without interpreting them as lack of love for each other. Anger drops away when you are willing to allow separateness and different preferences. You no longer try to make your mate over to fit your own needs and specifications.

Your mate's anger may be a signal to you that you need to grow. It may be a signal that he needs to grow. It may be based on misunderstanding and miscommunication. It may reflect issues from his past or yours that you as individuals need to face and release. It may belong in another relationship or situation, perhaps at work with the boss, or with a friend. It may be an attempt to manipulate. It may signal a power struggle. It may be a cover for sadness and hurt. It may be a reaction to something he fears in himself.

The challenge is to listen carefully, openly, and nondefensively to what he says about his feelings in order to discover what a particular experience of anger has to teach you. In this way, you stay current and clear with each other in your relationship. Keeping current with each other is like paying bills on time and using cash for purchases. When you do so, you don't accumulate debts and mounting interest fees to add to the original cost of what you choose to buy.

In relationships anger is a signal that there is an opportunity at hand and a cost to consider. If you face your anger and confront the situation at hand, you take advantage of the opportunity to learn about each other, face anger and conflict, resolve the conflict, and release your angry feelings with forgiveness. This is like paying cash. You stay current with each other as you share experiences and deepen your relationship.

If you ignore anger, bury it, and pretend you have no conflict, you build a wall that begins to separate you from each other. This is like buying on credit. In the short run, you get what you think you want; the illusion of peace between you. In the long run, you accumulate debt after debt with interest added as time moves on. In the end, the price you pay may be the relationship itself.

The fearful thinking Internal Saboteur tells you anger and conflict will destroy your relationship. It encourages you to ignore conflict and add brick after brick to the walls you are erecting between you. Paradoxically, these walls you create to protect you from conflict, destroy your relationship in the long run. They lead to separation and divorce unless you take them apart piece by piece, express the anger you buried in their creation, resolve the conflicts they represent, and release your anger with forgiveness.

The fearmongering Internal Saboteur is the culprit. It uses fear of separation fed by fear of anger and conflict to create the dreaded outcome and destroy your dreams. Only by becoming aware of the Saboteur and learning to say no to its destructive suggestions, can you release your fears and face the real issues that arise in an intimate relationship. Saying no to the Saboteur and yes to being honest with each other enables you to nurture your relationship successfully. When you stop allowing the Saboteur to paralyze you with fear, you have the strength to face the situations you encounter sharing your life with your mate. In the process, you become closer and closer to each other with every conflict you face. Anger is your friend when you choose to face it, learn from it, and let it go quickly.

It is easy to say you want to express anger appropriately and effectively. But how do you do that? Here are some guidelines to consider.

1. Learn to recognize your angry feelings when you have them.

2. Ask yourself if you are really angry or if your anger may be covering hurt or sadness you don't want to face.

3. If it is anger you are feeling, accept your anger without judging yourself for feeling it.

4. First, express your anger privately, by saying how you feel when you are alone and can vent your feelings without attacking anyone else. Or write about how you feel. You may or may not share what you write with the other person involved.

5. Give yourself time to get clear about what your anger is telling you. What, if anything do you need to do to take care of yourself in this situation? Have your boundaries, values or a personal commitment been violated in some way? If so, what is the real issue here? What is the bottom line?

6. Decide what you want to say to the other person involved in this situation. Again, practice saying what you feel and taking full responsibility for your feelings. Tell that person directly. Avoid creating a triangle by telling someone else and bringing a third party into the situation you're facing.

7. Pick your time carefully. Ask the other person if he is free to talk now or if another time would be better. Settle on a convenient time for both of you. Before you begin, be

sure you are centered and clear about what you want to say.

8. Make statements like, "I feel angry about this and I want you to know how I feel." Remember that you are not trying to change this other person. Your goal is simply to let him know how you feel and what is important to you in your relationship with him. How he responds is up to him.

9. Avoid unfair tactics like blaming, pleading, analyzing, labeling, preaching, moralizing, interpreting, diagnosing or telling him how he feels or how he should feel.

10. Be clear and specific about what you want. Leave him free to respond as he chooses. This is not about controlling him. It is about sharing what is important to you. You might ask him to simply listen to what you have to say and tell him you will be glad to listen to him when you have finished.

11. If he becomes defensive, tell him it isn't necessary to defend himself. He is not being judged or attacked. You just want him to hear what you have said. Avoid becoming defensive yourself. No one is on trial. It isn't a question of who is right and who is wrong. Both of you are okay. You are two separate beings who may have experienced and perceived something quite differently. You are simply sharing your different perceptions.

12. Stick to your point. Don't be drawn off into arguing about other issues that really aren't related to what you want to communicate.

13. When you have finished saying what you have to say, release the situation, thank him for listening and let your anger go. There is no need to hang on to resentful feelings. They harm no one but you.

The less you fear anger and the less you fear expressing how you feel, the less anger you will feel. You were taught to try to live life without anger in the first place. But this desire grew out of fear of that monster emotion. Life with a minimum of anger comes about only when anger is mastered, not when it is repressed.

When you accept anger as a natural part of your human experience, you find a friend you can allow to teach you and help you grow as an individual and in your relationships with others. As you overcome your fear of anger, you move closer to accepting all of who you are and all of who others are too. With growing self-acceptance comes a growing acceptance of others. The more you are able to accept all of who you are, the less anger you feel toward others. Other people no longer mirror rejected aspects of yourself, thereby stirring up your anger.

As you learn to center and accept all of yourself in unconditional love, anger gently drops away. You no longer fight with "what is". You accept "what is", trusting yourself and your spiritual resources to handle whatever the present moment presents and to move on to the next moment and its challenges.

In the next chapter we will explore this centering process, the key to nurturing yourself to success.

EXERCISES

Think of a situation that you feel angry about in the present. Practice telling the other person how you feel. First tell him in an attacking blaming way. Then center yourself (see Chapter 8) and tell him in owning language from your heart how you feel and why (e. g. "I felt angry when

________________ because ________________ . I would

like ________________ and I need ________________ .")
Notice the difference in these two experiences.

Be aware of the hurt you may uncover beneath your anger.

Allow yourself to acknowledge and express those feelings as well.

Release your feelings now and affirm that you are doing so in love and forgiveness. Let the situation go. Visualize your anger leaving your body and evaporating as it goes. Experience the lightness and relief that come with letting go.

CHAPTER VIII

CENTERING YOURSELF

Successful self-nurturing begins with developing an aware state of mind that enables you to notice your internal thinking, feeling, choosing and experiencing. This aware state of mind is called "the Higher Self", "the Central Self", "the Witness", or "Aware Consciousness". Whatever name we choose, we are referring to a process, not a static entity.

Aware consciousness is the process of noticing and observing yourself moment by moment throughout your life. This consciousness notices without judgment and evaluation, without comparison to others, and without any need for intellectual understanding or emotion. Aware consciousness is grounded in unconditional love. It does not have to control the outcome of what it is witnessing. It simply watches and notices what is.

You can focus your aware consciousness, deepen and enhance it, by learning to center yourself. This is a simple process that is intuitively familiar. At first, it requires full concentration. Gradually, this becomes a natural, simple response available anytime there is stress or a sense of being off-center. Knowing how it feels to be centered teaches you to recognize when you are off-center, so you have the choice of intentionally centering yourself again.

You may want to read through the description of the centering process that follows and then close your eyes and allow yourself to go through the experience. If you have trouble remembering the whole process, you can tape record the directions and then listen to your tape to guide yourself. Be sure to read slowly as you make your tape so you will give yourself enough time to fully experience each step.

First, feel for the center of your physical body by straightening your spine and moving your torso, feeling for a centered position, so you are not leaning off to one side or forward or backward. If you are standing, make sure your knees are relaxed, hips tucked in slightly, and body weight balanced on both feet. Then notice your breath, making sure it is flowing openly, so you are exhaling completely and inhaling fully. Your eyes can be closed or open with your concentration focused in the area of your heart.

Visualize a beam of pure white light streaming down from above your head, entering your head through the crown. Experience feeling this white light-love energy flowing from the top of your head, down through the center of your body, and out through the soles of your feet, pouring down into the earth, cleansing your body and nourishing our planet.

Now focus your awareness in the area of your heart, at the center of your chest. Feel into your heart and open yourself to the flow of unconditional love. You may feel a tingling, vibrating sensation. You may feel great warmth, or even a cool energy. Discover how you experience the energy of unconditional love and mentally affirm to yourself, "I center myself in unconditional love".

Then imagine the white light in the earth beneath you becoming a system of roots, or a single tap root, extending down from your feet and reaching to the core of the earth, bringing you nurturing and stability. See your root system clearly and feel how it supports you. Mentally affirm, "I am centered and grounded in unconditional love".

Now spin this white light around your waist and down

to your feet, forming a cocoon enclosing the lower half of your body. Spin the cocoon from your waist up to enclose the top of your body. Visualize yourself surrounded in white light and mentally affirm, "I am centered, grounded and shielded in the energy of love."

Once you feel yourself centered, grounded, and shielded, open your awareness to the space around your physical body and attune yourself to your energy field. Feel into the vibration of love and white light surrounding your body. Feel this white light flowing all around you and through you, filling you with the energy of love and protecting you from any approaching negativity. See yourself beaming this love energy to others, through your eyes, your hands, your heart, and your thoughts.

Again, visualize the cocoon of white light that encompasses your energy field. Mentally, visualize that brilliant white light changing into pure, clear quartz crystal. See yourself enclosed within that crystal. Then look out from your place within the crystal and visualize a black arrow coming toward you. Watch as it comes closer and closer and notice that it stops as it touches the outer edge of your crystal shield. Watch as the arrow gradually changes from black to gray to pure white. As it loses all its color, it moves easily inside the crystal where it becomes crystal, too. Your crystal shield expands and enlarges as the arrow is assimilated.

Next visualize a flight of black arrows coming toward you from a great distance. Watch as they come closer and closer to the outer edge of your crystal shield. Again they stop as they touch the outer edge of your shield. Change the arrows from black to gray, and from gray to white. As the arrows become white, they enter your crystal shield and become crystal too. Your crystal shield expands and enlarges, just as you grow and enlarge your being through your every encounter with the challenges life brings.

CHAPTER IX

UNCONDITIONAL LOVE

Unconditional love is love without judgment, comparison, or the need for intellectual understanding. Unconditional love is the life force, the energy that moves within you and all around you. It is the energy of the universe.

Opening yourself to the energy of unconditional love is like opening a door into the space where the essence of your being vibrates. Unconditional love is the energy that resides deep within your soul.

Unconditional love links you with your Higher Self. It is your connection with Infinite Being, Infinite Wisdom, Infinite Intelligence.

Your Higher Self is an unconditionally loving awareness that is available to guide you and assist you whenever you open yourself to its presence in your life. It does not push or force you. It is merely present and available for you whenever you choose to come home into its embrace.

Unconditional love accepts "what is" and honors the free will you possess to chart the course of your own life. Unconditional love enables you to release the people you are closest to and allow them to lead their own lives. And unconditional love encompasses the necessity for boundary keeping and limit setting. It recognizes that each individual must find his own center and from that center maintain the boundaries that are necessary for him to live comfortably and successfully. It means saying both yes and no in your relationships with others. It means loving both yourself and the other person. It does not mean discounting yourself in order to accept unacceptable behavior from others.

When Heather's daughter, Chris, was 16, the two of them were locked into a painful battle with each other. Chris was angry, frustrated, and belligerent. Heather was fighting to hold the line with her daughter and maintain appropriate limits with her. The more Heather tried to be firm and loving, the harder Chris fought.

Heather was wise enough to realize that Chris's anger reflected rage she had buried years earlier when her parents were divorced. When Chris was angry with her mother, she fled to her father's home to enlist his support in her battle with her mother. Dad was glad for her turning to him and encouraged her fighting with Heather. Eventually Chris decided she wanted to live with her Dad.

For years Heather had feared this possibility. She had raised Chris and wanted to complete her job. She was devastated by the rejection she felt from her daughter and her ex-husband.

Heather was forced to search deep inside herself to face her pain. Through this experience she found the meaning of unconditional love. Loving herself meant knowing she wasn't the object of all of Chris's rage. Loving herself also meant she deserved a break from Chris's battling. Loving Chris meant knowing that Chris's current struggle was an important part of her growing up. Loving Chris meant realizing that her daughter needed to know her father better. Loving Chris meant releasing her to work out her relationship with her dad and her anger with both her parents for their divorce.

Loving Chris and herself meant letting go of Chris without allowing herself to interpret Chris's need for time with her father as a personal rejection. Loving Chris and herself meant not judging her or comparing her with anyone else's daughter. Loving Chris and herself meant releasing Chris without guilt and revenge. Loving Chris and herself meant letting go.

The next few months were lonely for Heather as she adjusted to life without Chris at home. Wisely she left Chris free to approach her when she was ready. Heather refrained from pushing Chris to visit her and talk with her.

After several months, Chris began to drop by to visit Heather. They talked and laughed and saw each other in a new light. Each felt stronger, freer, and more independent. From this strength, they were free to like each other and enjoy each other in new ways.

Eventually Chris saw her father more clearly and realized that neither he nor her mother was really the problem in her life. She began the growing up that means knowing her life and her choices are her own; her successes and her failures her own responsibility; her rage, the child in her fighting accepting that powerful, personal and individual responsibility for her life.

Six months later she moved back to Heather's home. Mother and daughter enjoyed a relationship that was transformed; not perfect, but radically different. Now love meant knowing that neither held the key to the other's happiness. Freed of that confusing burden, Heather and Chris were free to love each other without blaming, judgment, resentment and guilt. Having let go of each other and survived, they could now face each other with the strength each knew was her own resource and the unconditional love that allowed them to heal their relationship by releasing it.

CHAPTER X

FEAR: THE SABOTEUR'S DELIGHT

Fear throws you off center and out of balance. It convinces you that nurturing yourself by keeping boundaries and setting limits with others is dangerous. After all, if you take care of yourself and assert yourself in healthy ways, you'll probably be rejected and abandoned by the people who are most important to you. Fear reminds you that their love is tenuous and may disappear if you dare to displease them.

Fear is the dark side of life. It alerts you when you are in real danger and need to take action to protect yourself. It also absorbs your mind when there is no actual danger, encouraging you to create problems by generating frightening thoughts.

Fear is the energy behind doubt, abuse, destructive behavior and violence. It is the Saboteur's most potent weapon. When you are afraid, your thoughts and actions are distorted by the apprehension you feel. If you escalate your fearfulness by engaging in more and more negative thinking, you can throw yourself into a spiral of destructive behavior. Then you feel powerless to stem the tide of the terror you have allowed your internal Saboteur to create.

Caught up in this snare of your own making, it is easy to lose sight of your higher self and have difficulty stopping your negative thoughts and destructive behavior. You are off-center. Even though you may know you are off track, you may feel helpless to find the path back.

Fear teaches you to expect the worst possible outcome in any circumstance, to doubt other people and to doubt yourself. It requires that you submit to its assumptions and affirm the negative outcomes it predicts. It paralyzes you and keeps you stuck in painful situations you need to release.

Fear causes you to neglect acknowledging and respecting boundaries. It stops you from setting limits. It sabotages you by convincing you that if you don't indulge others in what they seem to want, they may reject you, leave you, or hurt you in some other way.

Fear leads you to take advantage of yourself. It drives you beyond the limits of your physical and emotional endurance because you are afraid you cannot succeed without suffering and overworking.

Because of fear you take advantage of other people. Fear believes you cannot be successful and self-supporting on your own. Believing this, you cling to people you imagine you need, discounting them and yourself in the process. You think you have to cheat to win because fear has convinced you that your personal resources are not adequate for the challenges you face.

Fearfulness is expressed in destructive behavior when you give in to the Saboteur. When fear is in charge, you allow your impulses to control you.

Fear sabotages your relationships when you accept destructive behavior in other people and support them while they hurt themselves and you in the process. Yet you think you are playing it safe by not taking the risk of saying no or withdrawing your support.

You project your needs and your resources onto other people when you are afraid. Because of fear, you take care of them or take advantage of them, ignoring what each of you can accomplish on your own.

When you are afraid, you move from the present moment into the future and predict trouble. Fear leads you out of the present into the past also, so you can remember old hurts and disappointments and nurture the expectation that these will be repeated in the future.

Center yourself when you realize you are frightened and the Saboteur is taking hold of you. Let fear be a signal that you have lost your balance and need to recenter yourself in the present moment.

Your center is always present and available to you. Think of this center near your heart. Picture the energy of love radiating out from this area in an ever expanding spiral that encompasses your physical body and goes beyond it into the realm of the etheric and spiritual dimensions. Affirm, "I now center myself" while picturing this magnificent spiral. Relax your breathing as you come back into the present moment and release the grip of fear.

At each moment in time you choose either to be centered in the energy of love or to be off-center, operating with your Saboteur in the energy of fear. No matter how many times you need to do so, you can choose love rather than fear and recenter yourself in that healing energy. In this way you let go of the fearful Saboteur's grip and release it, rather than clinging to it and intensifying its hold on you.

Arlene was an only child in a fearful family. Her parents were overly protective and did everything they could to avoid upsetting her. They expected her to protect them in return. This meant she should not do anything they might not like or approve.

In this family there was lots of worrying. Arlene's parents showed her how to worry about all the bad things that might possibly happen. This family viewed life as too hard and too difficult for people to bear.

When Arlene became an adult (chronologically), she was still a child emotionally. She had great difficulty dealing with the ups and downs of ordinary living. She worried over herself as her parents had done, and kept herself unhappy, frustrated, and frightened about most of what she did. She allowed her fears to control her and avoided taking steps that might have made her life more enjoyable and more successful. Always she was afraid she would fail.

As Arlene and I worked together, I insisted that she take responsibility for scaring herself by becoming the fear-producing Sabotaging part of herself. When she said, "It scares me", I asked her to change her statement to "I scare Arlene that . . ." Then she said, "I'm scared to do that", I asked, "How are you scaring Arlene?". By owning the fear-producing, Sabotaging part of herself and changing her language in this way, she became aware of her power; the power to either scare herself or reassure herself. Once she recognized her responsibility for her self-induced anxiety, she had a choice she hadn't seen previously. She could continue to scare herself, or she could encourage and comfort herself instead.

Gradually she began experiencing her strength. I was firm with her and refused to sympathize with her helpless, "poor me" statements. She learned to notice when she was getting out of the present moment to scare herself with either what had happened in the past or what might happen in the future.

A part of Arlene was very angry while she was making these changes. Her angry self wanted to be treated like the helpless child she'd always been. When I refused to play the complementary role by commiserating with her, she was furious to have to notice her game. Yet her anger was a break-through too. She needed the energy and power of her long-buried rage to free herself from the prison of self-sabotaging fear she'd lived in all her life.

CHAPTER XI

HARNESSING YOUR POWERFUL PARTS

When you are off-center, you have identified your whole self with an energy pattern, known as a subpersonality or an internal part, and allowed it to take charge of you. Each of us has many such parts. We develop these energy patterns in response to our life experiences. They are each related to our central or higher self whose function is to maintain aware consciousness in order to guide us, recognize, and accept our subpersonalities, set limits with them, and create harmony among them.

Nurturing yourself lovingly means learning to recognize, name, and accept the myriad parts of yourself, including your Internal Saboteur. The object is not to eliminate any of your parts, even your dark, difficult ones like the Saboteur. It is to know them all and take them into account in your life rather than ignoring them and allowing them to control you unconsciously in demoniac, destructive ways.

Each of your parts is a distinct energy pattern, with its own personality and belief system. Each can be named and easily recognized by the feel of its energy and its patterns of thought, feeling and behavior.

In myself, I recognize Fearful Martha who thinks negatively and relates to the world through the fears I learned as a child. The Saboteur in me delights in using Fearful Martha for his purposes. There also are Vulnerable Martha; Protecting-Controlling Martha; Silent, Secret Martha; Sensual, Sexual Martha; Martha the Martyr; Angry Martha; Warrior Martha; Critical, Driving Martha; Nurturing, Loving Martha; Playful Martha; Magical, Creative Martha; Martha the Mother, and Martha the Bitch, to name a few of my me's.

It's fun to recognize and name these parts of myself. And, I've learned that when, with aware consciousness, I can identify one of these parts when she comes on stage in my mind, I have a choice about whether or not I become totally identified with her.

When I am totally identified with a subpersonality, I am out of touch with the rest of myself. When the subpersonality I identify with is appropriate to the situation I'm in, such identification is useful. But, when Fearful Martha or Critical, Driving Martha come along, I don't want to become completely identified with these parts because usually they are not appropriate, helpful, or constructive.

Fearful Martha used to be a very powerful part of me. I came by her honestly because I was taught fear throughout my early years. Fearful Martha is a negative-thinking, fearful-feeling subpersonality. My Saboteur tries to use her to spoil my fun and pleasure when I am happy and truly enjoying myself. I remember the time I first saw and felt her clearly. I was allowing Fearful Martha to take me over and sabotage my happiness.

I had just bought a beautiful home at my favorite lake in Oklahoma. I was thrilled and excited as I sat in the living room, looking out at the lake, and imagining all the good times our family would enjoy in this wonderful new place. Suddenly, I felt my mood change. I recognized a voice inside me reminding me that my daughters were in Colorado, skiing with their father. Would they get home safely?, it wondered. Would they ever get to see and enjoy this special place? All the bad things that could possibly happen flooded my mind. I was spoiling my fun. Fearful Martha had stolen my joyous moment.

Then another part of me pulled back and noticed what had happened. My aware consciousness saw what was happening and saw without judging me. As I was able to separate myself from Fearful Martha, I saw the humor in my situation. I laughed at how creative I could be at spoiling my own fun and scaring myself unmercifully. I also realized how Fearful Martha reminds me of my parents and my Southern roots. "Expect the worse and you won't be disappointed," was our motto.

By being able to see her clearly, name her, and love her compassionately, I began to gain mastery of Fearful Martha. She rarely is able to spoil my pleasure now. Yet, she is still within me and gets my attention periodically, especially when I am ready to take a risk and venture into totally new territory that will open new doors for me in my life.

One of her recent strong appearances came as I was about to board a plane for Hong Kong on the first lap of a trip around the world. As I walked toward the boarding area, I felt Fearful Martha stirring. She didn't want to go. She was sure something terrible would happen. She knew I would never be the same after this trip if I survived it at all. How could I leave my daughters so far away?

As I've taught myself to do, I centered myself and said "hello" to her; I acknowledged that I knew she was frightened; and I told her I would take good care of her. I also set limits with her. I reminded her that she is not allowed to take over and take charge of me. She is not allowed to spoil my fun. I told her firmly that we were getting on the plane and we were going to enjoy this marvelous adventure. And I did.

Being able to center myself in this way makes my life easier and more fun. Through centering, I find my strength and use it to take responsibility for coping with whatever situation life presents. I use my strength to set limits with the Saboteur and the parts of myself that can be troublemakers. I do not have to allow them to create problems for me, spoil my fun, or sabotage my life.

When you recognize your various subpersonalities, you create new choices for yourself. By taking this step up in consciousness, you can watch your parts in action without becoming completely identified with any one of them. This gives you a powerful new way to nurture yourself.

For example, if your Internal Critic is busy making disparaging remarks about you, questioning your worth and your competence, you can tune in with your Aware Consciousness and recognize the voice and the energy of your Critic. Once you are aware of what your Critic is up to, you can decide whether or not you want to listen to what it has to say. If your choice is to set limits with the Critic by choosing not to listen, your Inner Child will be relieved and delighted. It hates being constantly criticized and put down. By setting limits with your Critic you nurture your Inner Child and create a more positive loving climate for it.

The point in knowing your internal parts is just that; knowing them. You are not interested in changing them. You do want to understand their attitudes, beliefs, feelings, and objectives. By knowing and accepting all of your inner selves, you stop patterns of self-rejection and experience the wonderful sense of wholeness and healing that come from embracing all of who you are. But to embrace all of you, you also must uncover the parts of you that you have rejected, forgotten, and hidden away deep inside you. These are your missing parts.

CHAPTER XII

MISSING PARTS

The higher self can also help us notice the parts of ourselves that are missing or rarely allowed to be active in our lives. We may fear certain parts and try to live as if these potentials do not exist within us. For example, a person who appears to be always strong, in control, and unemotional may have cut himself off from the vulnerable part of himself. This part still exists and operates within him, but he does not take it into account. He may have convinced himself that he is beyond vulnerability, that he is safe and in control. Even though his vulnerable part is operating outside his awareness and may be creating sickness, confusion, and anxiety, he is out of touch with this dimension of life that affects every human being. One day he will find himself faced with tragedy, loss, illness, or some other major change in his life. Such an experience will challenge him to reown his vulnerable child self and care for it in a loving and compassionate way.

Our missing parts, operating as they do outside our conscious awareness, sabotage our lives in powerful ways. The person who is unaware of his vulnerability may ruin his health by pushing himself beyond the limits of human endurance. People who disown their angry parts leave these powerful energies to operate outside their conscious awareness and control. Their unacknowledged anger gets expressed in unconscious, underhanded ways that play havoc with business and personal relationships. It can also create depression and destroy physical health.

Suppose "the bitch" self is disowned in a woman. She does not recognize and use that energy when she needs it to protect herself in her interactions with others. However, in the privacy of her home, this unrecognized part may come out in mean, petty behavior with the people she loves most. She also may find herself attracted to men who are difficult and selfish. They have no trouble owning "the bastard" part of themselves and mirror this energy for her. She wonders helplessly how such a nice person as she could get involved with such impossible men.

When we ignore a part of ourselves, it is irritated with us, just as we are irritated when someone we know ignores us. If we ignore it enough, it will create disturbances until it gets our attention. For example, if the playful, fun self is completely overshadowed by the hard-working, driving part, we may get sick or find ourselves having intense and unreasonable rows with people we love and have no desire to hurt.

Other people notice these inactive or absent parts of us, too. They experience us as not being available in those ways with them. For example, if we are unwilling to be patient and loving with ourselves, other people will see us as impatient and hard or cold with them, too.

Nurturing yourself to success means recognizing and owning all of your various parts, even the ones you find most distasteful and frightening. The more of yourself you embrace and know, the less likely you are to undermine yourself with destructive behavior that operates outside your awareness and conscious choice.

Alyse came into therapy suffering from extreme anxiety attacks. Her home had been destroyed in a tornado several months earlier. With her remarkable ability to take charge of any difficult situation, she had managed to continue her busy schedule, working and being a homemaker and mother, while moving her family of five and supervising the reconstruction of their home. She was pushing herself harder and harder to stay in control even under these extremely difficult and challenging circumstances.

The harder she pushed herself, the more anxious she became as the vulnerable, frightened, overwhelmed part of her threatened to break into her awareness. She was terrified of this vulnerable part of herself and felt anxiety whenever this part came close to emerging.

As we worked together, I asked Alyse to become aware of the Protector-Controller part of her and then to move to a different chair in my office where she could be this part. When she moved, I acknowledged the Protector-Controller and thanked her for speaking with me. I explained to her that I knew what a good job she had done over the years keeping the Vulnerable Child in Alyse safe by hiding her away deep inside. I explained to her that perhaps her job could be easier in the present if she would allow Alyse to be in touch with this beautiful Child part in her. I assured the Protector-Controller that we simply wanted to get to know this Child; we were not trying to change her or get rid of the Protector-Controller. She shared with me her concerns about letting us talk with the Vulnerable Child and then agreed to the experiment. I then invited Alyse to focus on the Vulnerable Child within her and to move to yet another chair when she felt the presence of this child. She moved, and though it was difficult, finally this part of her was able to speak. Vulnerable Alyse was exhausted, frightened, and angry. She needed comforting. She had been completely ignored in the aftermath of the tornado.

Ironically it took this major disaster to finally force Alyse to face her vulnerable self and begin to reintegrate this rejected part of herself into her life. Without this human, sensitive, beautiful part of herself, she was missing out on much of the pleasure, beauty and joy in living. She had been trying to be a human machine. Now she could begin to allow the soft, gentle, vulnerable dimension of herself to balance her powerful, capable side.

EXERCISE: GETTING TO KNOW ME

Take a few minutes to have some fun getting to know some of the parts of yourself. The parts listed below are only a few of your available parts. As you become more aware and attuned to your own internal experience, expand the list to fit your needs. The more you can recognize and set up communication with all the parts of yourself, the more they will come into harmony and cooperation with you.

Talk to each subpersonality as though it were a whole person with needs, feelings, power, responsibilities and a contribution to make to the fullness, safety, and harmony of your life. Actually visualize it as a person. Ask each personality what it needs from you to work in greater harmony in your life. In your imagination, visualize giving that part of you what it needs. For example, the fearful part of you may ask for security and protection. You might see this part of you as a small child that you wrap in a blanket and rock in a rocking chair. Assure that part of you that you can and will take care of it. Thank it for alerting you to potentially dangerous situations so you can handle them adequately and protect yourself. Let it know that you love this part of yourself but will not allow it to control your life. You might even tuck it into a safe little bed.

As you begin to communicate with each part of you, pay particular attention to how each part feels. Notice how you experience its energy. Get a sense of the feel of its energy. This will help you to recognize this part easily when it comes into play in your life. You may want to take action to satisfy the needs of the various parts you explore. For example, you might take a warm bath to nurture the vulnerable child or get your desk organized to satisfy the part of you that needs organization and clarity in your work.

Here is a way you might begin your dialogue:

Hello, fearful ________________ *(use your name). What do you have to say to me? What do you need from me? What do you have to offer me? How do you behave when I ignore you?*

Thank you for serving me by making me more aware of your role in my life. I will take care of you by ________________

____

____

And in return I want you to ________________

____

____

Hello, Saboteur in ________________

Hello, Playful ________________

Hello, Creative ________________

Hello, Critical ______________________________

Hello, Worrying ______________________________

Hello, Protecting, Controlling ______________________

Hello, Vulnerable ____________________________

Hello, Pushy ________________________________

Hello, Powerful ______________________________

Hello, Warrior ______________________________

Hello, Pleaser ______________________________

Hello, Sexual ______________________________

Add your other parts as you become aware of them.

You may want to read an excellent book about your various parts. *EMBRACING OUR SELVES* by Hal Stone, Ph.D., and Sidra Winkelman, Ph.D., is a manual for learning to dialogue with the selves within you. It was published in 1985 by DeVorss and Company, P. O. Box 550, Marina del Rey, California 90294.

CHAPTER XIII

CENTERING AND PHYSICAL HEALTH

Your physical body reflects the harmony or disharmony that exist within the orchestra of your subpersonalities. Accepting and loving your subpersonalities and acknowledging their feelings will enhance your physical health and well-being.

Before I learned to notice and acknowledge my subpersonalities and their feelings, I suffered from a variety of physical problems; headaches, an ulcer, colitis, fatigue, insomnia. Now at forty-three, I am much healthier than I was at twenty-three. I rarely experience physical problems or illness. When I do, usually I have ignored my vulnerable self and her feelings and needs over a period of time. Being ill used to be the only excuse I allowed myself for taking a day off from work or taking time to rest. As I have learned to relax and enjoy leisure, I don't hesitate to give myself time off to balance work time with relaxing time. I no longer push myself until I'm sick in order to take a break. I respect my limits and the necessity for balance in my life.

When illness does occur it is important to accept the illness and surrender to the physical body's needs for rest and healing. Being sick is not a sign of weakness or failure but a signal that we need a quiet time to regain balance in our lives. We may be experiencing a cleansing process after making profound shifts in consciousness. Illness may signal the necessity for a radical change we have been avoiding or denying. The rest we are forced to take gives us time to contemplate what we have been ignoring in our lives. When we recognize where the imbalance is and decide how to correct the problem, healing is usually rapid and complete. The illness is a necessary experience and a useful, cleansing process. It helps us find our center again.

Frequently, illness reflects a problem with saying "no" to other people. Without this choice available to us, we may exhaust ourselves and our resources doing what we don't really want to do. Eventually the physical body cries out as if to say, "Hey, you, watch out. You're hurting us and not even caring how we feel. We may just check out of here if you don't wise up." If our body gets our attention and we take steps to correct our problems and express the feelings we've been ignoring, the illness will no longer be necessary. It will clear up and our health will be restored.

CAROL'S STORY

Carol was a woman about my age when I met her eight years ago. She came to me after learning that she had breast cancer that had metastasized. As we became acquainted, I learned that both her parents had died of cancer in the past five years. She had cared for them during their illnesses.

Carol had three teenage children and a two-year-old daughter. The baby had not been planned and had come soon after another pregnancy that ended with a stillborn child. Carol had never talked about or even acknowledged her feelings about the baby she lost or the one she now had. Nor had she allowed herself adequate expression of her feelings during her parents' illnesses and deaths.

In addition to her family responsibilities, Carol worked a night shift at a local electronics firm to augment the family income. Her marriage was strained; she carried the lion's share of household responsibilities and rarely allowed anyone else to help her.

As we talked about her life and her illness, Carol acknowledged that death was the only way she could see to get herself out of her present difficulties. She made it clear to me that she wanted help for her family, but she had little hope or desire to make the changes that would be necessary if she were to clear up her problems and transform her life.

So I worked with Carol and her family to help them face her illness and learn to talk, share, and support each other through this painful experience. Carol's transformation came through death a year later. Her family's transformation came through sharing Carol's dying and learning to express the love they felt for her and for each other.

BEA'S STORY

Bea's story has a different ending. Bea developed cancer when she was in her early 30's. Her response was to fight for her life with all her resources. In the process, she had to face all of herself, including the part of her that wanted to die. She decided to make major changes, including a divorce from her husband of 15 years. They had four children.

As Bea searched her soul and faced the ways she had ignored her own needs, ignored her talents and creativity, ignored her feelings about her marriage and ignored her anger with her demanding and sometimes insensitive husband, she knew what she had to do. And she had the courage to make the changes she needed. She had the courage to face life single with her four children and cancer. She decided to live and live in tune with herself and her needs.

Now fifteen years later, she's a healthy, happy woman. She lives in a different city, is married to a different man, and enjoys writing, illustrating, and publishing books for young people. Her own children are successful and happy, too.

Illness signals us that we have been sabotaging our lives in some way and need transformation and cleansing. Transformation can come through deciding to live or deciding to die. That choice is one that only can be made by the person who is ill.

Maggie Creighton, director of the Cancer Support and Information Center in Palo Alto, California, says to her cancer patients, "I have two hands. With one I can help you to live. With the other I can help you die. The choice is yours and either choice is OK with me."

This is unconditional love. I love you and work with you, releasing you to your own choice about the ultimate outcome of what we do together. I respect the boundaries that define each of us as individuals. Though my own desire may be that you choose to live, I realize that the choice is yours, not mine. I love you either way.

CHAPTER XIV

CENTERED THINKING

Nurturing yourself successfully requires an unconditionally loving consciousness and a clear-thinking mind that also is centered in love. With your mind and through your thoughts, you direct your energy and your life. Moment by moment you choose your thoughts; either loving, positive, affirming, and encouraging thoughts or fearful, negative, discounting, discouraging, self-sabotaging thoughts. The thoughts you energize depend upon which of your parts or energy patterns you choose to embrace.

Negative thinking is the Saboteur's delight; a disease that consumes lives as destructively as cancer. It directs energy in negative patterns, creates painful emotions as a result, and leads to destructive behavior that harms the physical body.

Nurturing yourself to success means being aware of the thought patterns your various parts energize. Through aware consciousness you create choices you didn't have before. This allows you to choose positive, loving thoughts and refuse to energize negative, fearful thought patterns.

You can redirect your life by choosing your thoughts and working with statements that affirm that what you want to create for yourself is already true. Affirmations are thoughts that are statements of will and intention designed to direct your life and channel your energies in positive, loving and enhancing ways. Making affirmations is like programming a computer. By using affirmations to program your mind positively, you claim the power you have to create your own reality and make yourself happy and successful.

You may not have noticed the power of your negative affirmations. Perhaps you sometimes hear yourself affirming, "I'll never get this done"; "I just can't lose weight no matter what I do"; "He'll never stop drinking"; "I always feel depressed on Sundays"; "I could never make that much money". Somehow we don't connect our negative predictions with the negative outcomes we experience.

When I began to work with positive affirmations, I noticed for the first time how many negative thoughts I had been energizing. These negative thought patterns had a powerful impact on my life.

When I was a child, I was told, "Don't get your hopes up. You'll just be disappointed." "Hope for the best, but expect the worst" was another powerful statement that I heard often. I learned to dread being disappointed. If an outdoor activity was planned, I knew there would be rain. If a trip were planned, maybe something would happen to prevent it. The possibilities for worry and negativity were endless. And when a negative prediction materialized, I certainly hadn't seen the power of my thoughts in creating the very reality I feared. Now I realized I had best stop my Internal Saboteur and heal myself of the negative thinking disease, which was destroying my life.

Limit setting is just as essential at the mental level of consciousness as it is at the emotional and physical levels. When I say no to a negative thought and immediately replace it with a positive affirming thought, I re-center my thinking and claim my strength, power, and responsibility for my thoughts and my life.

Claiming this power and responsibility is growing up, realizing you can do and be whatever you are willing to invest yourself in doing and being. Growing up in this way is recognizing and releasing the helpless, victim parts of yourself and the critical, negative-thinking parts that hold you captive, a victim of your own Saboteur and its unnoticed negative mental processes. Growing up in this way is recognizing that through your beliefs and your thoughts you create your own reality.

Mystic wisdom schools teach that there are many planes or levels of vibration in the universe. The highest vibratory levels of manifestation are the divine. The lowest level is the physical dimension in which we exist. This is the level we perceive through our five senses. The plane next above the physical is the emotional; the third plane is the mental; the fourth is the intuitional. The intuitional plane links the lower vibratory levels of manifestation with the higher spiritual dimensions of consciousness.

The physical dimension is the plane of effects; those effects reflect causes or direction from the higher vibratory levels. The emotional dimension creates effects in the physical dimension. The mental dimension directs both the emotional and physical dimensions. The intuitional level links man with God and is the dimension of wisdom, spiritual direction, insight, and unconditional love. In our lives in physical form, we encompass these four levels of manifestation. As we are able to see how these vibratory levels affect us, we can gain direction and guidance from higher realms of consciousness.

During my early adult years I experienced many physical problems. At that time, I was completely unaware of the power of the emotional and mental levels in my life. I existed at the physical level. I knew the spiritual level was of great importance to me. But I had no sense of connection between my physical reality and God. I did not see how the love of God could heal my life. I had no sense of how God's love filters through my higher dimensions of consciousness to permeate my thoughts, my emotions, and my body.

When I learned to meditate, I experienced a dimension of consciousness and a peace I had not known before. I realized that no matter how difficult the circumstances, if I could meditate, I could find renewed strength to cope with my life. I was beginning to experience reconnecting my physical reality with God's love as I learned to quiet my body, my emotions, and my mind and attune myself with higher levels of awareness.

Since that beginning I have found ever-expanding sources of peace and guidance for my life. And step by step I have learned how the spiritual, mental, emotional and physical levels of being connect my life with God's love and direction.

You can heal your mind through meditation and unconditional love. When you infuse your mental processes with the energy of the heart, love directs your life. You set your intention for your life through the thoughts you think. Your thoughts are reflected and manifested in your life through your emotions and your body. By transforming your thinking through the energy of love, you transform your life.

Affirmations are an essential tool in this transformation process. There are many wonderful books on the power of affirmation. I have listed my favorites at the conclusion of this chapter. I am sure there are many others I have yet to discover. Catherine Ponder's books give example after example of how people have healed their lives with affirmations. I read and reread these books to strengthen my mental programming.

And I have learned to work with affirmations in my own ways. At first, I simply thought an affirmation. Then I learned how much more powerful the affirmation is as a directive when it is spoken aloud and written as well.

One evening during a group session, I asked each participant to meditate and ask for an affirmation to work with during the coming week. Later we shared the affirmations that came to each of us. Mine was, "I am blessed, healed, and prosperous in all aspects of my life."

Before I went to sleep that night, I wrote this affirmation several times (10 to 15 is an effective number) and said it aloud a number of times as well. During the night I awoke briefly and heard the words, "It is time to stop drinking coffee." I went back to sleep immediately. When I woke up the next morning, I stopped consuming caffeine. Though the five or six days following that change were unpleasant as my body detoxified, the effort was well worth the results. Now, a year and a half later, I am calm, relaxed and more consistently peaceful than I ever remember being before that change.

I am sure my work with my affirmation triggered this healing in my life. And I know the power of my mind repeating the affirmation gave me the strength to stay with my resolve to release caffeine through the first few difficult days.

The key is to make an affirmation, say it aloud, and say it in three different voices. (I, Martha, am lovable, successful, and prosperous. You, Martha, are lovable, successful, and prosperous. She, Martha, is lovable, successful, and prosperous.) You will also want to write it a number of times each day and repeat it whenever a negative, contradictory thought enters consciousness.

As you work with your affirmations, release the outcome. Don't try to force and control your process. Make your commitment to follow the steps that come into your awareness as guidance from your higher dimensions of consciousness. When you work consistently in this way, your life will be enriched in amazing ways.

Paradoxically, love and positive, loving thoughts help to surface fear and negativity that have been buried deep inside. When you use affirmations, your fearful, negative thought patterns will come into your awareness. This is one of the most interesting phenomena associated with the affirmation process. Sondra Ray in her book, *I DESERVE LOVE*, suggests an exercise that is very helpful for working with these negative thoughts.

Take pencil and paper and divide a page into two columns. In the left column, write an affirmation for yourself. Continue writing the affirmation and listen for any negative thoughts that rise to the surface. List those negative thoughts in the right-hand column. Continue the process for as long as negative thoughts continue to arise. Then write your affirmation a number of times after you have exhausted your fears.

Here is an example of an affirmation I worked with in this way. Notice how a resolution begins to occur toward the end of the process. Since doing this exercise, I have had no difficulty continuing the affirmation without negative interference.

AFFIRMATION	NEGATIVE THOUGHTS
I am lovable.	
I am lovable.	I'm not lovable.
I am lovable.	No one really loves me.
I am lovable.	People only love me if I help them, if they need me.
I am lovable.	If they really know me, they won't love me.
I am lovable.	Don't get your hopes up.
I am lovable.	I have to work hard for love.
I am lovable.	Why not me?
I am lovable.	Maybe it is possible.
I am lovable.	God loves me.
I am lovable.	Yes!
I am lovable.	
I am lovable.	

These are some of my favorite affirmations which I have

gathered from teachers, the books on affirmations that I recommend to you at the end of this chapter, and created for myself.

I deserve love.
I am love.
I am lovable.
I never lose anything that is for my highest good.
Telling the truth always heals.
I create beautiful surroundings for myself.
I listen to my own wants and needs and respond generously to myself.
I talk to myself lovingly and gently.
I give thanks for all the blessings I experience today.
I appreciate myself and encourage myself frequently.
I am blessed, healed, and prosperous in all areas of my life.
I attract loving friends.
I give love freely and am open to receive love from everywhere in the universe.
I am now willing to receive love, support, and money from everywhere in the universe.
I love you. I bless you. I release you. May our love allow us both to become all we are created to be.
I trust myself and empower myself.
I give thanks for my perfect health and well-being.
Everything I eat nourishes my body and is perfectly assimilated by my body without adding any extra weight.
I give thanks for accomplishing the goals I have set for myself today.
I love my life and every day I live.
I salute the divine in everyone I meet.

These are excellent books about the affirmation process.

I DESERVE LOVE by Sondra Ray, published in 1976 by

Les Femmes, Millbrae, California.

THE DYNAMIC LAWS OF HEALING by Catherine Ponder, published in 1966 by DeVorss & Co., P.O. Box 550, Marina del Rey, California 90291.

THE PROSPERING POWER OF LOVE by Catherine Ponder, published in 1966 by DeVorss & Co., P.O. Box 550, Marina del Rey, California 90291.

REBIRTHING IN THE NEW AGE, by Leonard Orr and Sondra Ray, published in 1977 and 1983 by Celestial Arts, Berkeley, California.

THE ONLY DIET THERE IS by Sondra Ray, published in 1981 by Celestial Arts, P.O. Box 7327, Berkeley, California 94707.

LOVING RELATIONSHIPS by Sondra Ray, published in 1980 by Celestial Arts, Berkeley, California.

PROSPERING WOMAN by Ruth Ross, Ph.D., published in 1982 by Whatever Publishing, Inc., P.O. Box 137, Mill Valley, California 94941.

OPEN HEART THERAPY by Bob Mandel, published in 1984 by Celestial Arts, Berkeley, California.

SUBLIMINAL TAPES are also a marvelous resource for healing your mind. I have used them with great success for the past eighteen months. Because they require little effort to use and because they communicate directly with the unconscious mind, they are an important tool for creating healing change. Obviously it is crucial that these tapes be well prepared and carefully selected. I recommend the wide selection of tapes published by Midwest Research, Inc., 6515 Highland Road, Suite 203, Pontiac, Michigan 48054.

CHAPTER XV

FOOD, WEIGHT AND LIMITS

Eating well is a crucial aspect of nurturing yourself successfully. Yet our cultural lack of adequate skills for healthy self-nurturing is painfully obvious in this area of our lives. The Internal Saboteur plays on our fears about food, our emotions, and our physical bodies. It takes advantage of our deeply-held, negative beliefs about food, feelings, and beauty. Many of these beliefs are based upon misinformation. We fail to see how affirming these beliefs creates the predicted outcomes we dread.

Ours is a fat-conscious society where people spend millions of dollars every year in efforts to lose and control body weight. Obviously something is wrong when so many people struggle with their bodies in this way.

We believe food can do more for us than food is intended to do. Mothers feed crying children before making any effort to comfort them in another way. A child cries; he gets something put in his mouth. His mother is afraid of emotions, afraid of comforting him with her body, with her emotional warmth and calmness. She may be upset herself. She has learned to eat when emotions frighten her. She teaches her child to do the same.

Food becomes more than nourishment for the body when we add the emotional dimension to its role in our lives. The connection between physical hunger and eating blurs. Emotional hunger becomes a signal to eat, too.

We fail to limit food to its intended function in our lives when we add emotional soothing to its role. And we create a trap for ourselves. Eating is a temporary diversion from emotional experience. It does not really satisfy emotional needs, but it does distract us from uncomfortable feelings, temporarily. We may continue eating and eating in a costly attempt to avoid feelings we fear. We would be much better off to release our fear of feelings and have a good, cleansing cry or express our anger in a healthy way or let ourselves have genuine pleasure.

Facing feelings and then releasing them clears us of situations that are completed. We then have nothing left to avoid; we don't need distractions like food, alcohol, drugs, or overworking to keep us diverted from the emotional dimension of our lives.

When we use food for emotional soothing, we also forget that food and healthy eating are essential to health and well-being. Nurturing yourself successfully includes feeding yourself lovingly and well. It is OK to eat. It is necessary to eat. There is no need to be in a constant internal battle about food.

Of course, the Saboteur loves to create guilt about eating. Its strategy is to criticize eating patterns no matter what those patterns are. This persistent criticism generates a rebellious response in return.

Have you ever had an internal exchange like this while going through a cafeteria line?

The Saboteur: You can't have anything sweet to eat. You're on a diet. You look terrible. You've got to stop making such a pig of yourself.

The Rebel: I'm sick of all this pressure. Just watch me have this piece of pie. You can't make me be so perfect. I hate you!

Inevitably the rebel wins sooner or later. The net result

is that the Saboteur manages to undo what may have been a healthy commitment to stop eating sugar. Notice that the Saboteur's first move is to make a comment that appears to be supporting that commitment. As soon as it has your attention, it moves in with a barrage of critical, negative comments calculated to hook the rebellious child.

It is at this point that recognizing the Saboteur and saying no to it are essential to nurturing yourself successfully.

Let's go back to the cafeteria line.

The Saboteur: You can't have anything sweet to eat. You're on a diet. Of course, you never do very well with diets and does it ever show. Just look at that fat face. How do you think anyone could like you looking like such a slob!

Aware Consciousness: That's the Saboteur, criticizing and preaching.

Internal Nurturing Parent: I don't have to listen to that. I have set a goal for myself to stop eating sugar. I feel better when I keep that commitment. The pie isn't worth the price I'll pay for having it. If I'm really hungry for dessert, I'll have an apple.

Internal Child: (Relaxing). I feel good and loved when she stops that mean voice. I don't really want pie. An apple might be good. I'll see how I feel after I eat lunch.

Notice how simple it is to say no as soon as you spot the

Saboteur at work. The end result is relaxing and affirming. There is harmony rather than confusion and dissension. The Inner Child begins to trust the Internal Nurturing Parent to take consistently good care of it. In such a loving environment, it feels safe and sane. The child is satisfied, having its hunger acknowledged and being fed in a healthy way.

Overeating and gaining weight are ways the Saboteur uses to keep us like children, helpless and rebellious. This is a powerful strategy for hiding your sexuality, attractiveness, and personal power from yourself and from others. Unconsciously you may hide your attractiveness and power to protect your parents, yourself, and other family members as well from their fears of your growing up and leaving them.

In some families obesity is the norm. The family myth is that fat people are nicer, better, more fun. The implication is that a slender person wouldn't be welcome and acceptable in this family. Being fat is a way of belonging in the family.

These patterns are marked by powerful spirals of negative, fearful thoughts and beliefs. Negative affirmations abound. "I can't lose weight; I try every diet, nothing works; I'm hopeless; what can I do. It doesn't matter what I eat, I gain weight just looking at food." Weight is an obsession and negative thinking nails its creator into a prison of fat she feels powerless to release.

How many times have you heard your Saboteur say, "You shouldn't be eating this; it's going straight to your hips. You'll end up getting fatter and fatter." And then the rebellious child retorts, "But I just can't help myself. It tastes so good and I'm so tense right now. I'll just have to go on a diet later." Look at what you set in motion if you don't recognize and stop the Saboteur at this point. These powerful affirmations work so well it's easy to forget how you let the Saboteur image and create extra pounds for you.

Nurturing yourself successfully means claiming the power you possess to stop the Saboteur and affirm health and balanced body weight. Center yourself in the energy of love and make positive affirmations. "My body is now adjusting to my ideal weight." "I give thanks that I now weigh 125 pounds." "I release all excess weight and appreciate my complete healing of all desire for unhealthy foods." "The food I eat is assimilated perfectly by my body. I never gain weight no matter what I eat."

These affirmations may heal weight problems if they are practiced consistently and used to replace the Saboteur's negative thoughts as soon as they emerge. The key is centering the mind in the energy of love, making a commitment to be the size you want to be, and claiming your power to stop the Saboteur and think in a new way. Risk affirming that the goal you have set for yourself is already accomplished.

Because energy follows thought and commitment, your behavior reflects your mental processes and the content of your thoughts. Positive affirmations keep your thoughts centered in love and focused on your commitments to yourself. They program you to desire healthy food and exercise. They program you to set limits with yourself without setting up power struggles and self-defeating behavior. Positive affirmations program positive, constructive behavior.

For most of my life I have believed that I would never be fat or gain excess weight. I have often said, "I never gain weight no matter what I eat." There have even been periods in my life when I tried to gain weight but with little success.

In my early thirties I was close to a friend who worried excessively about what she ate. I began to absorb her fearful attitude about "forbidden" fattening foods. My Saboteur found a new weapon. For the first time in my life,

I found myself gaining weight and worrying about what I ate. My Saboteur told me that because I was getting older I was now susceptible to what my mother used to call "middle-age spread". I set up a vicious circle of thinking that spoiled my pleasure and ease with food.

After several years battling food and constantly monitoring my weight, I realized I was allowing my Saboteur to program me with outmoded beliefs about the inevitability of gaining weight as I grew older. When I recognized what I was creating, I learned to stop the Saboteur and change my thinking. I readopted my old affirmation, "I never gain weight no matter what I eat." Food dropped back into a reasonable, centered position in my life and my weight restabilized at the level I desire.

EXERCISE:

Ask your aware consciousness to notice what you tell yourself about food and eating. Then jot down the beliefs and affirmations you uncover. Next change each negative statement into a positive affirmation you want to empower in your life. Now select one of your positive affirmations. Write it in the left-hand column on a page divided into two columns. In the right-hand column, record the negative reactions that arise in you as you write your affirmation again and again. Continue to write your affirmation until you have exhausted your negative reactions to it. (See Chapter 4 for an example of this process.) Repeat this process with other affirmations. Whenever you become aware of your Saboteur thinking an old negative thought about food, say no to the Saboteur, release that thought, and replace it with one of your positive affirmations. Congratulate yourself for your new awareness and responsibility for the thoughts you empower.

These are excellent resources for making peace with food.

THE ONLY DIET THERE IS by Sondra Ray, published in 1981 by Celestial Arts, P. O. Box 7327, Berkeley, CA 94707.

Midwest Research, Inc. Subliminal Tapes, 6515 Highland Road, Suite 203, Pontiac, Michigan 48054

Tape #1	Weight Loss
Tape #45	Body Toning Through Mental Imagery
Tape #64	Psychoneuroimmunology
Tape #47	Developing a Winner's Attitude
Tape #63	Personal Power Dynamics
Tape #14	Getting It Done! Stop Procrastination!
Tape #7	Overcoming Fear and Worry
Tape #65	Relieving Anxiety

CHAPTER XVI

TIME, MONEY AND BOUNDARIES

Just as eating well is essential to nurturing yourself adequately, managing your time and money effectively are also crucial skills for success. The Saboteur loves to use fears about scarcity to deny abundance and prosperity and to fuel problems in managing both time and money. If we allow the Saboteur to control us with fearful thoughts of scarcity and lack, we create a constant struggle to have enough money and enough time to satisfy our needs. We battle with these elements of our lives and strive to overcome a constant deficit.

On the other hand, we can say no to the Saboteur's fear-mongering and instead perceive the world as part of a universe of abundance. There really are ample resources to meet our needs. A mental attitude of abundance transforms a miserly, self-defeating existence to a rich experience of the flow of giving and receiving the wealth of resources that are available to each of us.

Abundant thinking assures us that we have ample personal resources of strength, creativity, and intelligence. If we invest these personal resources in productive activity, we place ourselves in the flow of abundance. When we are giving the fullness of what we have to give, and are open to receiving in turn, we can trust that our needs will be met since what we have given comes back to us in another form.

The flow of abundance encompasses both giving and receiving. We must give of ourselves in order to receive. And we must be willing to receive in order to reap the fruits of our efforts. Our challenge is to take full responsibility for our talents, resources, strength, and intelligence and use them wisely to fulfill our life purpose. When we are giving fully of ourselves, we must also fully open ourselves to receive abundance and prosperity in return.

When we block our giving by clinging to the past, refusing to take full responsibility for our abilities, or waiting for someone else to be our caretaker, we experience a corresponding lack of abundance flowing back to us. When we are afraid to receive, afraid to open ourselves to the flow of love, support, and money from the universe, we also block ourselves from experiencing the abundance we deserve.

We encounter the ultimate form of balance through the universal laws of giving and receiving. We are each a part of the whole of the universe. When we fulfill our responsibilities and give unstintingly of ourselves, while also being open to receive from others, we are in harmony with the universal flow of resources and abundance. When we are hoarding our resources, talents, and money, and therefore blocking ourselves from both giving and receiving, we create disharmony, and interrupt the universal flow of resources and abundance.

The Biblical tithe, giving 10% of what we earn to the source of our spiritual enrichment, recognizes this flow. When we claim our responsibility for giving back to the universal source of our supply a portion of what we receive, we take our place in the flow of abundance. We recognize destructiveness of hoarding and greed. What we release through our giving comes back to us multiplied many times over so we may continue to return more and more for the universal good as we are more and more prosperous in all aspects of our lives.

Our time and our talents are our resources for investing in our lives. Our prosperity reflects the wisdom with which we invest these basics we all are given. We all have an abundance of time and of talent. Growing up is claiming that abundance, taking responsibility for our lives, releasing limiting beliefs that block our prosperity, and experiencing the joy of taking our individual places in the ongoing richness of life.

As more and more individuals take hold of prosperity consciousness and move into abundant living, our communities will experience a revival of prosperity and growth. When a city or nation is depressed economically, it is caught in the grip of fear. This fear is contagious and spreads through the culture, creating new and ever more serious economic problems. The economy is immobilized, people lose jobs, fear saps their creativity, they struggle to change their lives and may or may not manage to meet that challenge.

In a period of economic growth, fear is banished in an atmosphere of optimism and abundance. There is a lively excitement pulsing in the air. Anything is possible.

As long as we imagine we are at the mercy of the economy as a whole, we fail to see the power each of us possesses to create prosperity in our own lives no matter what the larger economic picture happens to be. When we can see the power that rests in our creativity, we know we can find a way to succeed whenever we choose if we fully tap into our capacity for creative problem solving.

As more and more individual family economic units become clear about money, prosperity, and abundance, the larger economic picture will reflect a new stability based on enlarged understanding rather than fear or exaggerated optimism. The economy as a whole is the aggregate of all the individual economic units that exist within it. When we educate ourselves about money and prosperity and teach others what we learn, we help build a more stable economic base for everyone.

Each of us as an individual holds the key to financial success in our own life. As we claim that power and responsibility, we make choices that will benefit others and our community as a whole. And we can create networks of people with complimentary skills and interests to stimulate larger and larger gains for ourselves and the community as a whole.

It's all a matter of claiming our enormous creative powers and trusting ourselves to follow the guidance we receive and the opportunities that open for us. We are limited only by constraints of time, space, and available energy, our archaic belief systems about ourselves and life, the rejected and disowned parts of ourselves, (especially the Saboteur), and unresolved conflicts from past experiences. As we unravel our limiting and outdated belief systems and work to revise them, we open ourselves to go beyond old boundaries to experience new vitality and success.

Centering ourselves in the energy of love and moving with the universal laws of giving and receiving bring us abundance that is beyond our conception. But when we ignore limits, ignore our resources, and defy the laws of the universe, havoc and chaos rule our lives, wasting our resources, and generating scarcity of time, money, love, and support.

As we learn to center ourselves and shape our lives with balance we form boundaries that are appropriate and necessary for our health and well-being. We create an environment for ourselves that enables us to fulfill our life purpose and goals. And as we accept the limits of life in this dimension and the universal laws of giving and receiving, we free ourselves of the self-sabotaging prison of rebellion, frustration, and inertia that hold us when we fight accepting what is and struggle to control what we cannot control. Through accepting and embracing our limits, we actually open ourselves to move through barriers and beyond our boundaries to experience unlimited abundance and prosperity.

EXERCISE:

Take pencil and paper. Give yourself about five minutes to list your 10 favorite pleasures. Center yourself, relax, and let your ideas flow.

Now star your favorite pleasure. Center, relax, and list 10 ways you could make money while enjoying this favorite pleasure.

If you want to continue this creative exploration, list 10 ways to make money from each of the other pleasures on your list.

At this point, you may want to set some goals for yourself and write those goals in a list that you will work with regularly (daily or at least once a week). Feel free to revise your list of goals as you move along, discovering what works best for you in the process. Be aware of two levels of goals as you work with your list: the large, overall intentions you are setting for yourself, and the small steps that are necessary to move toward those objectives. You may want to set up your goals' list with several major intentions and steps toward those intentions listed as subcategories.

For example:

My Goals for 1986

A. To complete this book and write another.

1. Set aside time each day for writing, preferably two hours each morning.

2. Share what I have written with friends for feedback and comments.

3. Research the advantages of self-publishing vs. finding a publishing company.

4. Complete the final draft of this manuscript.

5. Decide how to publish and market this book.

6. Get it done!

B. To continue to develop and improve my radio program, SPEAKING OF LOVE, LIFE, AND SEX.

1. Continue to work to improve my voice and my ability to relax and be myself on the air.

2. Develop new ways to publicize the program and develop the listening audience.

3. Read new books and articles regularly to continue my learning process and help me be a better resource for listeners.

4. Continue to develop and maintain a good working relationship with the radio station and our sponsors.

5. Listen to tapes of the broadcast each week to evaluate my work and learn to be more effective with people.

These excellent books are resources you may want to explore:

MONEY IS YOUR FRIEND by Phil Laut, published by Trinity Publications, 1636 N. Curson Avenue, Hollywood, California 90046.

YOU CAN HAVE IT ALL by Arnold M. Patent, published by Money Mastery Publishing, Box 336, Piermont, New York 10968.

THE DYNAMIC LAWS OF PROSPERITY by Catherine Ponder, published by DeVorss & Co., P.O. Box 550, Marina del Rey, California 90291.

CHAPTER XVII

KEEPING BOUNDARIES AND SETTING LIMITS

Road signs mark city limits and state lines that divide one governmental and cultural entity from another. We see these boundary lines on maps. But the map is not the territory. Boundary lines on maps are abstractions, created to give us a picture of the way we divide and identify the land where we live and travel. These imaginary lines do not actually exist on the land itself unless the boundary line is also a river.

Other kinds of boundaries are easier to see. A physical boundary separates one person, object, or area from another. It is easy to see an object like a table, and to see clearly where the table is and where it is not. Its boundaries are obvious.

The physical body is a separate and distinct entity, too. It is easy to see where one person's physical body ends and another's begins. But, like lines on a map, emotional and mental boundaries between people are abstract. They are subtle and easily confused because of the complex ways we communicate and interact with each other.

Transactional Analysis draws a picture of a person with three ego states; Parent, Adult, and Child. These three ego states, represented by three circles, drawn like a snowman, are enclosed by a line that encompasses all three. This line represents the boundary that defines one human being and separates him from another.

We can add the Higher Self to the Transactional Analysis diagram of a person.

The Higher Self is available and ready for you whenever you release your breathing, relax your physical body, and sense into your higher dimensions of consciousness and wisdom.

With the Higher Self in the picture, we must separate the Nurturing Parent part of the Parent ego state from the Critical Parent part. We also must distinguish the Free Child part of the Child ego state from the Adapted Child part. Since the Critical Parent and the Adapted Child both operate in the energy of fear, the Saboteur, not the Higher Self, directs them.

The Nurturing Parent (NP) part of the Parent ego state flows directly from the Higher Self. The Nurturing Parent relates to the Free Child (FC) within you and calls it forth to enrich your life with fun, creativity, spontaneity, and joy. In the presence of the Higher Self, the Adult ego state is a centered, clear-thinking resource for directing your life.

(PA = Positive Adult).

The Critical Parent (CP) part of the Parent ego state flows from the energy of fear and carries out the Saboteur's directives. It parents you with critical, judgmental, negative messages and relates to the Adapted Child you create in response. The Adapted Child helps you survive in the face of this negative, fearful energy. The Adapted Child is careful, fearful, defensive, ashamed, and shy. In the presence of the Saboteur, the Adult ego state is an off-center, negative, and confused thought source, (FA = Fearful Adult).

Two people in a relationship are pictured as two separate entities, each with a boundary defining his space.

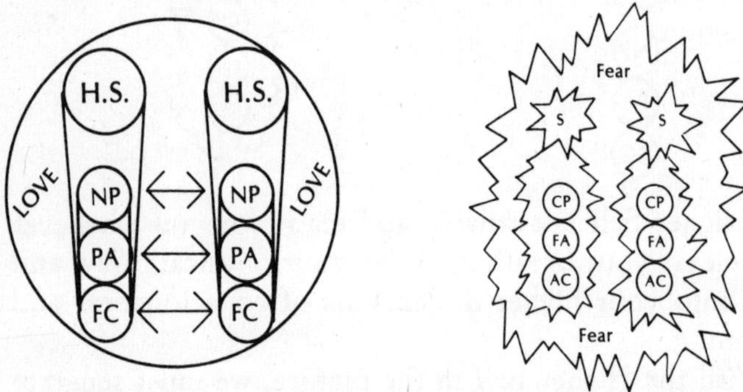

Setting limits means drawing lines in our relationships with others to maintain the integrity of the emotional, mental, and physical boundaries that separate one person from another. (At the same time, we also honor the spiritual level of being, where in the highest sense, we are all part of an infinitely greater whole.) It means we say no when we want to, and we are honest and have the courage to relate to others openly and lovingly. Setting limits enables us to be in charge of ourselves and take full responsibility for the integrity of our own lives.

Within the confines of our outer boundaries, there are also boundaries that define our internal parts or subpersonalities. The Transactional Analysis model recognizes three such parts, the three ego states, with further subdivisions within the Parent, Adult, and Child. Other therapy models, like Psychosynthesis and Voice Dialogue, recognize many more parts within us. No matter what model we adopt, boundaries are crucial to delineate these separate parts so that the central aware Higher Self can direct our lives by setting limits with our various selves, and not allowing any one subpersonality to take over and dominate our lives.

Setting limits within yourself and with other people helps you stay clear about your power and responsibility to yourself for the way you live your life. Setting limits allows you to keep healthy boundaries both inside yourself and in your relationships with others.

You set limits when you say no to another person's intruding into your personal space. You also set limits when you say no to yourself and resist the temptation to intrude into another person's space. The third arena for limit setting is within yourself when you say no to a subpersonality that may be attempting to take you over and sabotage you in some way.

Accepting the existence and usefulness of boundaries between people creates freedom. It means taking yourself into account in your relationships so you don't get caught in the trap of "loving others too much". Fighting against boundaries locks you into rebellious behavior that drains your energy, your resources, and your health. Boundaries make life simpler. Setting limits keeps relationships constructive and healthy. Boundaries give definition and structure to your life so you can be in contact with others and live with them in peace and love.

Keeping boundaries helps you stay centered. If you go off in all directions, individually and in relationships, you are like liquid with no container to hold and shape it. Without boundaries for definition you are easily pulled off-center. You are not whole. You are out of touch with your real self; out of balance, not integrated. Without boundaries you have difficulty focusing your attention and accomplishing your goals. You tend to focus your energy on taking care of others and trying to control their lives while ignoring your responsibility for your own. Setting appropriate limits creates self-respect and helps you stay centered. It helps you claim all of who you are and experience yourself as a whole human being. It stops you from loving others too much.

Boundaries are the way you know who and what you are and who and what you are not. Boundaries help you distinguish what is "you" from what is "not you". When you can make this distinction, you free yourself from the confusion of living as if you can be responsible for someone else.

A marriage in which both partners are able to live and breathe and function as separate and equal individuals, will be a marriage that stays healthy and grows stronger with the years. Both partners can live and grow in the balanced environment they create for themselves and each other.

But if in a marriage, relationship, group, or business, one person invades his neighbors' space, pushing their needs and interests aside and escalating his feelings and needs over theirs, a cancer begins to form that may ultimately destroy those relationships. When this occurs, the invaded people have failed to maintain the integrity of their own boundaries and responsibilities. They have failed to say "no", to hold their own ground, to fight back to preserve the integrity of their own needs, goals, and desires.

This is like a failure of the immune system in the physical body. Without adequate protection from invading germs or runaway cells, the body will be overcome by disease. When we fail to give ourselves adequate protection, power and potency in our dealings with others, we leave ourselves open to being hurt or destroyed in cancer-like relationships.

Both the aggressor and the invaded party are hurt in such a relationship. Both are engaged in destructive, boundary-denying behavior that poisons their association. Both suffer in the process.

Cancerous relationships can be cured by restoring healthy boundaries between the individuals involved. Healthy relationships will stay healthy if healthy boundaries are maintained.

When we allow our limits and boundaries to be violated, we make ourselves too open and too vulnerable. When we love others too much, the people we allow to invade us mirror our own Saboteur. Because we haven't yet learned to stop its destructive activities within us, we attract other people into our lives who reflect the Inner Saboteur we fail to acknowledge and master. Often we are just as blind to the destructive patterns in the people we allow to use and abuse us as we are to our own. We fail to provide adequate protection for ourselves and our own interests. We allow ourselves to be overwhelmed by forces that are external to us. We feel like victims, hurt, betrayed, bewildered. How could anyone treat us this way?

Of course, the answer is that we have failed in our own responsibility to ourselves. We fail to see our own Saboteur and how we allow it to control us. We neglect saying no to the Saboteur that is within us as well as to the person outside us who mirrors its disregard for our own well being. We cannot expect other people to look out for our interests any better than we do ourselves. When we abdicate responsibility for ourselves and take on responsibility for others instead, we open ourselves to being a victim.

Some people are especially vulnerable to allowing their boundaries to be violated. Adults and children who have experienced childhood sexual, emotional, and physical abuse have distorted perceptions of boundaries between people. Because their bodies and emotions were violated and abused, they learn to discount and ignore their boundaries just as their adult abusers did by invading them emotionally or physically when they were children.

Incest and other abuse survivors have a special challenge in learning to recognize, respect, and maintain adequate, healthy boundaries for themselves in relationships. They also must learn to respect other people's boundaries so that they do not expect too much from others.

Failing to maintain adequate boundaries sets the stage for the Saboteur and makes his work easy. You may not set limits within yourself so that you over-indulge in food, alcohol, drugs, sex, work, play, negative thinking, or spending money. You may not set limits with other people so that you do what you don't really want to do, fail to say "no" when you should, distort and deny your needs, and make decisions that are destructive to your own interests. You may use and abuse other people, failing to notice that their acquiescence will be costly to your relationship in the long run. You may then be surprised when that other person finally reacts by severing your relationship. The outcome could be divorce, loss of a job or promotion, or loss of friends.

Conrad was a "spiritual teacher" who challenged others to transcend their limitations in order to experience abundant prosperity and wealth. While part of his message was valid and useful, it was clear that Conrad's own finances were not as healthy as they should have been if his principles were workable.

Conrad, in his zeal to overcome limitations and limiting beliefs, virtually ignored boundaries and limits between people. He started his classes late, took breaks that were twice as long as scheduled, and did not cover the content material he promised in his seminar sales brochure. He took little notice of the people he taught.

Because he ignored the boundaries between himself and other people, he discounted their time, their expertise, and their expectations of him. Consequently, he created an irritated audience, and undermined his effectiveness as a teacher. Ignoring limits does not overcome limitations. Conrad's failure to accept reasonable boundaries created limitations on his effectiveness as a teacher despite the fact that he was an excellent, witty, and articulate speaker.

The common denominator shared by all kinds of self-sabotage patterns is a violation of boundaries and limits. Nurturing yourself to success means learning how to keep boundaries and set limits effectively.

CHAPTER XVIII

BOUNDARY KEEPING IN RELATIONSHIPS

Respecting boundaries allows you to know and love others without fear of consuming or being consumed in the process. Relationships with healthy boundaries enrich your life and enable you. Relationships that ignore keeping boundaries and setting limits are marked by fear, anger, resentment, and guilt.

Let's look again at the traditional Transactional Analysis model to help us understand boundaries and limits in relationships. TA draws a picture of one person incorporating three ego states; parent, adult, and child. The parent nurtures, protects, criticizes, and judges. The adult thinks and solves problems. The child is the emotional, feeling, intuitive, creative part of a person.

Notice the boundary that surrounds this person. It is the line encompassing the three ego states.

Two people in relationship are drawn with a boundary encompassing each one.

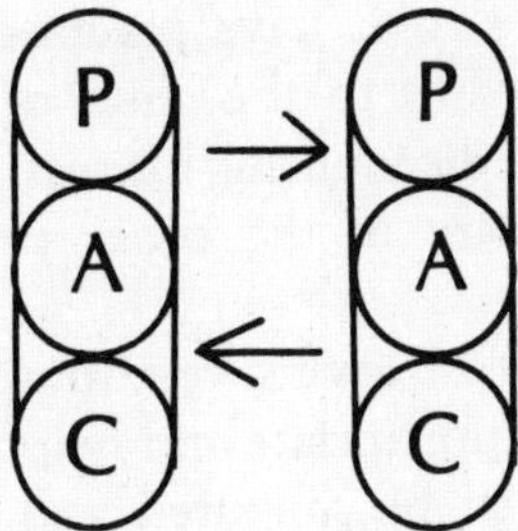

With these boundaries in place, each person sees the other as a whole, capable, and competent. Each person has available, and can use, all of his parts to function effectively in the world.

Yet people in relationships frequently form what is called a symbiosis. They live as if one could not function or survive independently of the other. A symbiosis looks like this:

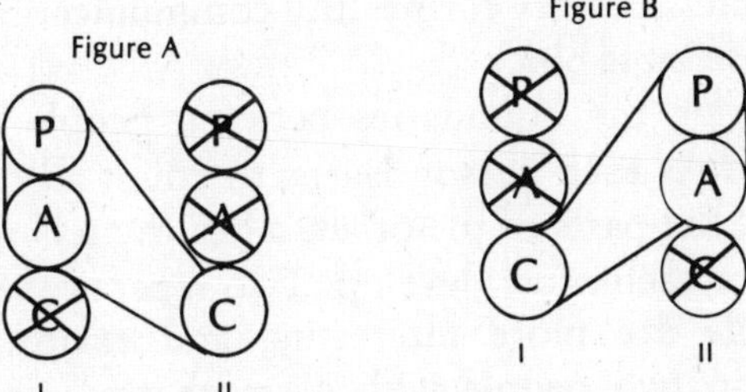

In Figure A, Person 1 acts as parent and adult for the child of Person 2. Person 1 discounts the child in himself and the parent and adult in Person 2 in order to do this. Person 2 is discounting his own parent and adult parts and the child of Person 1. Consequently, these two people are functioning with only half of their available resources. The boundaries between them have faded and they behave as if they were one. All of this is based on discounting the wholeness of each other and allowing fear to dictate in the guise of loving concern.

In Figure B, the roles have reversed and Person 2 is being parent and adult to the child of Person 1. In the process, Person 2 is discounting his own needs and feelings in order to take care of the other person's needs and feelings.

There are times in loving relationships when such a symbiosis may be appropriate and helpful. In a crisis, one person may need to be nurtured and protected by the other. In other circumstances, these roles will reverse.

But in the ordinary course of living, symbiosis stunts the growth of both people involved, and cripples their relationship. In marriages, this crippling often is reflected in a poor or non-existent sexual relationship. When boundaries between people are ignored and lost, the exchange of energy and excitement between them is impoverished. The relationship becomes sticky, held together by the glue of unexpressed anger, resentment, and guilt. The free, open interaction necessary for healthy communication and sexual expression is blocked.

Restoring the boundaries between people heals relationships. As each person learns to count all of his parts and all of the parts of the other, a healthy self-respect and respect for each other develop. Two separate, self-respecting people are more interesting and exciting to each other than two people with a smothering grip on each other can be.

Kahil Gibran in *The Prophet* describes this loving attitude of separateness and release in a relationship "Love one another, but make not a bond of love . . . let there be spaces in your togetherness . . . Sing and dance together and be joyous, but let each one of you be alone . . . stand together yet not too near together."

CHAPTER XIX

BOUNDARY KEEPING WITH MATES

In order to experience being centered with your mate, you must respect the boundaries that define you as separate beings. When you are able to center yourself and fully accept the boundaries that define you, you can experience an energy and a connection between you and your mate that transcends your separateness and enlarges your lives and your relationship.

Knowing your center, you also know your boundaries and limits. And, respecting your boundaries by maintaining limits with yourself and with others, brings you into a deeper and deeper experience of centeredness. Centering and limit setting are reciprocal and essential to a healthy marriage.

Limit setting with mates is a particular challenge for it is coupled with the task each mate faces of loving and accepting each other as each person truly is. How do you balance your own needs and preferences with accepting your mate's behavior or communication patterns that may offend you?

Both of you are adults, and each of you has his own values and standards. You cannot expect to make your mate over to fit the mold you create for him. Obviously, you both will win when you communicate honestly with each other so you can find mutually acceptable solutions where conflict exists. Honest communication also helps you find shared values that both of you can accept.

Yet, even when you communicate well, there still is a human tendency to push each other to discover where the limits and boundaries are in your relationship. Each of you needs to let the other know when a boundary has been crossed and a limit violated. The issue is communication, not an attempt to punish or control each other. Each of you needs to know about the values that are important to the other.

Ideally each of you will modify your behavior to respect your partner's preferences where those preferences are reasonable and healthy. Both of you will recognize the importance of adjusting to each other's needs and preferences so you will nurture your relationship and allow it to grow.

But it is easy to allow fear to take control instead. In the name of being autonomous, you may refuse to consider your partner's needs and preferences. You may be afraid you will be allowing your mate to control you if you honor his requests. Actually it is fear, not your mate, that controls you. And you are the one who surrenders to fear.

Fear also is reflected in critical, judgmental behavior between you. Criticism and personal rejection poison your relationship and set up deadly competition between you. Your battling with each other mirrors your individual, internal struggles among your various subpersonalities. When you heal yourself with unconditional loving acceptance of all of who you are, you will find little use spending your energy judging and criticizing your mate.

But with fear in control, it is easy to disown responsibility for your thoughts, feelings, and choices. How many times have you heard yourself say, "He makes me so angry!"; "She took advantage of me."; "She makes me feel terrible."; "He hurt my feelings."?

These statements are our culturally sanctioned copouts, and they are especially popular between mates. In your marriage, it is convenient to see your responses to your mate's behavior as beyond your control. You may have learned from early childhood to believe others are responsible for your feelings, your thoughts, and your choices. If so, you don't experience that you have a choice about how you react and interact with others. Yet you make these choices constantly whether or not you are aware of your process and whether or not you take responsibility for what you choose.

If your mate is angry with you, your angry part will be aroused also. How you handle your angry self will depend upon your level of awareness and the choices you make out of that awareness. You can choose to allow your angry self to take you over and take charge of you. If you do this, you may fly into a rage and tell him off. Since he's already angry, you will probably have a difficult scene. If you are aware of your anger and choose to acknowledge it and accept your angry self while keeping your higher self in charge of your behavior, you may choose not to respond to his anger. You may simply do nothing, and in that way, allow him to process his own feelings without the confusion of yours thrown into the situation. Later you may tell him about your response to his behavior.

Fear also can lead you to ignore blatant violations of your own needs and preferences. If you fear angering your mate, it is easier to keep the peace than to speak honestly with him about your needs and feelings. This pattern is a disservice to both of you. Your mate needs to know you respect yourself enough to speak honestly when something happens that is a violation of your principles. You may choose not to respond to minor irritations, allowing your wisdom to guide you about what is truly important and what is merely a preference. But when the issue is a major one, like honesty between you, emotional or physical violence, or abuse of drugs, alcohol, or money, you need to take a stand.

It is not loving to either of you to ignore such major issues. Both of you need to look at your responsibility in creating such problems. And both of you need to commit to resolving your contribution to creating these destructive patterns. If these issues are ignored, they will spread like cancer and destroy your relationship unless profound healing occurs.

It is helpful to distinguish between what you cannot live with if you are loving with yourself, and what may be simply critical, distance-making behavior. Honesty, nonviolence, and nonabuse of drugs and money are essential for a healthy relationship. These are bottomline, basic issues which determine the strength of the foundation upon which your relationship rests.

At another level, resting upon this foundation, you deal with your personal needs for stroking, affirmation, and encouragement. When you are truly loving and nurturing with yourself, you are free to empower your mate as you express your love for him through thoughtfulness, generosity, kindness, loving words and behavior, and sexual sharing and intimacy. But where there is fear of closeness, many distance making patterns will appear. The game, Blemish, described by Eric Berne in *GAMES PEOPLE PLAY*, is played to avoid closeness by finding fault with someone else in a nitpicking way. If you are constantly busy finding fault with your mate, you spoil your pleasure in being together and block feelings of closeness. Fear of closeness creates many unnecessary barriers between mates. But fear of closeness and distance-making patterns are not lethal. You can learn to change these patterns with relative ease.

At the third level of issues, you encounter personal taste preferences like taste in homes, clothing, foods, neatness, entertainment, relaxation, intellectual and spiritual commitments, and style of life. These are important bonds in your relationship. Where you share many interests and preferences, your relationship has lots of strengths to build upon.

When there are problems in your marriage, it is helpful to identify the level at which these problems exist. If most disagreements are at the personal taste and preferences level, your relationship still has many basic strengths. Creative compromises and mutual accommodations usually are possible with the development of good communication skills.

Problems at the second level require that you open yourselves more fully to allow the flow of love energy between you. You need to learn to nurture yourselves more completely as individuals and as mates. Each of you must make peace with yourself, realizing that the quality of your relationship reflects the depth of your self-acceptance and self-esteem. As mates you must learn to give and receive positive strokes. You also need to be more fully expressive of your thoughts and feelings and able to share more of yourself with your partner.

Problems at the foundation level require serious effort and merit serious concern. They reflect abusive parenting experienced as a child and require intensive personal therapy to heal. Help from an experienced therapist-teacher is essential.

Good communication and good will are crucial in solving problems at all three levels. When you realize that a loving relationship brings each individual's issues and fears to the surface to be faced, it's easy to see how important it is to both partners to grow through the rough places you inevitably encounter. When problems begin to surface in a relationship, it's smart to seek help from a therapist-teacher. Taking this step early, before your relationship is seriously damaged can save years of pain and dissatisfaction. It also helps you develop nurturing skills which will enrich and strengthen your relationship and pay dividends for years to come.

In learning to set limits effectively with your mate, it is useful to be aware of the degree of difficulty a particular issue represents. You can accommodate and be understanding about differences that involve personal taste preferences and the open, free-flowing expression of love. Here there is room for lots of give and take and understanding.

But at level one, you encounter the bottom line. The issues here are much more serious. You cannot afford to overlook their importance. Effective limit setting is essential if your relationship is to grow in a healthy direction. If one of you chooses to ignore and discount these bottom-line issues, the other may have to choose to leave the relationship. At this level, unconditional love for yourself and for your mate precludes tolerating dishonesty, violence, and drug or money abuse. Here the only loving answer is "no" even when that means your relationship cannot continue.

As you learn to say "no" in a loving and effective way, you can also say "yes" and allow real closeness and intimacy in your life. When you have mastered letting go of others and freed yourself of the illusion that you can control them, you are able to take hold of your own life and take charge of what you can control; yourself. You are free then to pursue your life goals and release other people to their own responsibility for their own lives. When you release and let go in this way, you relax with the deep knowing that what is yours will come back to you; that what is not to be in your life will be removed. For you never lose what is for your highest good.

Letting go in this way recognizes that life includes periods of loss, change, and reintegration. Life is a cycle of changes reflecting the passage of time and the constraints of space and distance.

You marry and release your original family ties to establish the primary bond in your life with your new mate. Time passes; your child is born. Now you are no longer a couple only. A family is created. Perhaps other children are born. Your first child begins school. Teenage years approach. You realize your children are growing up. High school comes and high school graduation. Your oldest child leaves home. The others grow up, graduate, leave home, come home and leave again. They marry and release you as parents. You are now a couple again. Mother's life role is no longer primarily mother. What will she do with the rest of her life? Father faces similar questions about his life. Will he retire or will he begin new ventures in his later years? Meanwhile your parents have aged and sometime in these years death confronts your family. Spiritual questions become more and more important as the meaning of death and life must be faced if growth is to continue. Physical death is the ultimate limit you encounter living in this dimension of time and space.

Each of these experiences presents you with a myriad of challenges as the passage of time confronts you with the limited duration of each phase of life you encounter. You are constantly challenged to release one phase in order to be free to move on to the next. You constantly face these limits. You have to say "good-bye" to what you are accustomed to and greet a whole new set of challenges as you move ahead.

As you accept the limits inherent in all relationships you realize that you are born and you die as an individual. You meet and touch many other lives as you move through your life experiences. You say hello and good-bye. You are close and you let go. You have the resources you need to face the challenges life presents. You have the strength to meet these challenges alone and in relationship. You are whole. In relationship you expand your possibilities.

Yet in a healthy relationship you know that your partner does not hold the key to the meaning of your life. You hold that key yourself. Your mate is a blessing. Your mate enriches you. Your mate does not eliminate the challenge before you to find and fulfill the purposes of your life.

Relationships are best when you know your own strength and purpose and carry your own weight, respecting your partner's strength and purpose and allowing him to carry his own weight, too. Ballroom dancing expresses this principle beautifully. In order to dance well together each partner moves his own body. In dance, framing means giving your partner your strength to push against so the pair of you can move together in harmony. Each dancer is carefully tuned to the movement of the other as one leads and the other follows. Energy and excitement flow between two people dancing in connection with each other. Strength meets strength and creates a harmony that is more than the sum of the two individuals involved.

One person does not drag another's limp body around the floor if the dance is to be enjoyable and beautiful. One does not step on the other's toes. The dance respects limits, boundaries, and individual integrity and then goes beyond all that to create something more beautiful than either dancer alone can attain.

And then the music ends, the dance is over, and each dancer returns to his own space. You come together and you release. You breathe in. You let go. This is the rhythm of life. You are one. You are two. You are one again.

CHAPTER XX

LIMIT SETTING WITH CHILDREN

As a parent you want to love your children unconditionally. Yet how do you do this while also setting appropriate limits for them and keeping boundaries between family members clear?

Unfortunately many new parents have little or no preparation for the responsibilities of parenting beyond their own childhood experiences with their parents. Lack of adequate education for this enormously important life task, coupled with our human tendency to repeat abusive patterns if we have been abused, mean that dysfunctional family systems replicate themselves from one generation to the next.

If you were abused, emotionally, physically, or sexually as a child, you can stop these destructive patterns in your adult family if you are willing to look honestly at your feelings about your own childhood and learn to nurture yourself successfully. Only when you know how to take really good care of yourself will you be able to nurture your children as you genuinely want to do.

Nurturing your children to success means loving them unconditionally and providing an adequate structure of responsibilities, values, rules, and limits for them. An adequate structure of rules, responsibilities, and consequences teaches children eventually to structure their own lives, take care of themselves in the world, and set limits for themselves and with their peers.

In order to provide this kind of loving structure for children, parents must overcome their fears. Parental fears with children fall into two major categories. Parents are afraid of emerging autonomy, freedom, and separateness in their children. They also are afraid of their children's anger and possible rejection of them.

When parents are afraid of the autonomy and separateness of their children, they often resort to overly-restrictive, overly-punitive, and overly-protective behavior. They try to control their children's activities to lessen their fears of their growing up and becoming independent.

One family I worked with had told their 16-year-old daughter that she was not to drive her car beyond certain streets in the city in which they lived. Another mother insisted on knowing exactly where her teenage daughter was going and what she planned to do whenever she left home. In another family the teenage daughter was not allowed to attend parties with classmates because of her mother's fear that she would misbehave. This young woman made good grades in school, had been responsible for her younger brother after school for several years, and held a job successfully.

In all these situations, the restrictions were unrealistic, impossible to enforce, and encouraged rebellious behavior. The parents in each family complained that their daughters lied to them. The young women were in a terrible bind. "I can't tell the truth or I won't be allowed to do anything."

By the time children are 16 and have the privilege of driving, parents need to know they have taught them to behave responsibly and constructively. Ideally they have set appropriate limits, enforced those limits, and invoked consequences when those limits were violated. Through this process children learn to respect boundaries and to set limits for themselves.

When parents see clearly that the goal of parenting is to

prepare children to become responsible, independent adults, they teach their children to become self-sufficient so they will be able to survive on their own in the larger world beyond the family. When children who have been taught to take good care of themselves come of age, their parents know they can trust them. They are confident that their children will be successful as they venture into the world on their own.

Young people need this vote of confidence from their parents. They have their own fears to overcome as they begin to leave the comfort and security of home. They need to know that their parents who are so important to them believe they will make it and be successful with their lives.

They need to know how to say no to what is not in their best interests. They need to know how to handle money effectively. They need to know how to select clothing, care for their wardrobes, and do laundry. They need to know how to clean and create an orderly place to live. They need to know how to ask questions and find the resources they need for solving problems. They need to know how to drive a car and take care of it. The list goes on and on. They need to know how to be responsible for their sexuality.

Parents who are afraid have trouble preparing their children to be adults. Some parents have their lives so focused on their children that the prospect of their growing up is too frightening to face and encourage. They may be afraid their children will love them only if they need them and are dependent upon them. They may think they have to control their children's lives because they dare not trust the choices they would make on their own. Fear keeps these parents from trusting themselves to parent successfully and then let go of parenting and move on with their own lives after their children are grown.

Overly-permissive, overly-protective, smothering behavior in parents reflects their fears and creates fears in their children. A sixteen-year-old girl told me how frightened she was of growing up. She was trying to blot out her fears with alcohol and drugs. She realized, "I don't even know how to make my bed. My mother has made my bed every day of my life." Her mother's need to be needed was disguised as thoughtfulness and helped to cripple her daughter. Fortunately this young woman was determined to learn for herself what she needed to know and today is doing quite well on her own.

Often exceptionally bright children do poorly in school because no one has the courage to stand firm with them. These children are clever at manipulating their parents and other authorities. The more they get away with, the more they are driven to push for limits with more and more provocative behavior. When they finally encounter someone who is prepared to be firm with them, they are relieved. The necessary structure of rules, limits, and consequences helps them learn to harness their energy and resources so they can use their powers constructively and successfully.

In other families, parents may be overly controlling and punitive with very bright children. These whiz kids then use their brightness to outwit their parents. They find excitement in getting away with breaking the rules.

This pattern is sometimes most clearly seen in adults who are the grown-up versions of these bright kids. They may become successful very quickly. Then they keep pushing for more and more — more money, more power, more success — until they overstep limits like laws, rules, financial realities or physical health needs. Ultimately they may be indicted by a legal body, file for bankruptcy, or develop a serious or fatal disease. Had they found appropriate limits earlier in their lives, they would have been better able to handle success and intelligence and use it creatively and constructively. Their task as adults is to develop these skills on their own initiative.

When parents cater to their children's whims, they are

afraid of upsetting their children. These parents don't feel comfortable with anger and resentment. They are afraid of rejection, and they protect their children from the consequences of their behavior when they break rules. They try to keep peace at all costs. Young people raised by such fearful parents may emerge with no respect for adults, no respect for themselves, and an arrogant attitude that the world owes them whatever they want. Other children raised by fearful parents try to be perfect and live in fear of making mistakes and angering their parents.

When I was a child my parents set limits with me indirectly. Their aim was to keep me quiet, and they taught me to fear displeasing them. I was afraid of their anger and afraid of disappointing them. They told me they had sacrificed everything for me. The implication was that I should repay them for those sacrifices and feel guilty about what they did not have because of these choices they made.

I coped with this manipulative style of limit setting by developing a harsh, driving subpersonality that pushed me to be perfect at everything I did. Because I was terrified of getting into trouble, I did everything I could to insure that I pleased other people. I took few risks that might mean punishment. When my parents were displeased with me, they were rejecting and emotionally abusive. I did all I could to avoid being vulnerable to them in this way.

As an adult I have had to learn to say no to my harsh, critical demanding Pusher part that I developed in response to my parents. It is a tool of the Saboteur and a relic from the past. My parents used fear in their attempts to control me and my Pusher drove me with fear of displeasing others. My job has been to learn to set limits for myself in a healthy, loving way and to allow myself to relax and enjoy life.

Healthy limit setting occurs in a context of love, not fear. As a parent you are relaxed, confident of your parenting skills, and prepared to deal with your children appropriately as they move through the stages of childhood growth and development.

Infants need lots of warmth, nurturing, and physical comforting from their parents. They are adjusting to a strange new environment and are most comfortable close to the familiar older world of mother's body. With calm, relaxed, confident birthing and mothering, babies are calmer themselves. Tense, fussy babies reflect tense, anxious energy from their mothers and may have had difficult birth experiences as well.

During the early stages of her growth, the infant requires a great deal of care and nurturing. Limit setting is not yet an important issue. Creating a healthy, loving and centered bonding between the infant and its parents is the primary concern. Ideally the baby feels safe, senses that she is in good hands, and learns that her needs will be met. Her parents are not afraid to leave her alone in her crib after she has been cared for and needs to rest again. Her crying does not alarm them, and the baby learns to accept being put down to sleep.

As the baby begins to crawl, exploring the larger world is her mission. She is beginning to function separately from her parents and has everything to learn about the world she inhabits. Here the challenge of limit setting begins. Parents say "no" firmly in a strong but calm tone of voice, shaking their heads "no", and removing the baby from the danger she has encountered. If she goes right back to the forbidden object, they remove her again and repeat their firm "no". If another attempt follows, they can put the child in a more confined space where she will not be able to disobey again.

The key is calm consistency. That is a challenging demand for first time parents who are young and inexperienced. Yet parents can learn to parent well if they are willing to seek help from parenting classes and groups, books, their parents, grandparents, and friends. If they practice saying "no" consistently, and allow their child to experience the consequences of disobeying or ignoring parental directions, she learns that she can trust what her parents tell her. She experiences that "no" really does mean " no".

Hitting and spanking are not necessary if parents are skilled in limit setting. Parents who know and trust the power and force of their presence, their words, and their confidence do not need to resort to hitting to control a toddler. They can put the child in his play pen, or in his room as he grows older, to signal to him that his disobeying his parents costs him a measure of his freedom to move about. If spanking is used as a consequence, it is essential that the parent be in control of his own emotions so he does not become too intense or violent with his child. Resorting to hitting and losing control reflect powerlessness and frustration on the parents' part. It demonstrates to the child that he can throw his parents off center. It makes him feel too powerful and it frightens him too much. He learns to hit, too, when he is frustrated and angry.

As the child grows older, he can be required to stand in a corner when he is naughty. A corner is a good teacher for a child. The corner marks the intersection of the boundaries or walls that define the space in a room. Standing still, facing a corner, confronts the child with the reality of boundaries and limits. Parents require that he stand quietly for a defined time looking at the corner. This punishment respects the child's dignity, demands that he exercise self-discipline by being quiet and standing still, and lasts for a short, defined period of time which is measured by a timer with a bell. The time begins when the child has control of himself. He is not allowed to sit, scream, lie down, or fuss while his corner time is counted. Two or three minutes are long enough for a young child. Older children can handle longer periods and need more time to feel the impact and consequences of their misbehavior.

Effective limit setting with children includes an adequate overall time structure for their lives. Children feel secure and their needs are best met by a schedule that is predictable and clearly defined. Time to get up, meal times, nap times, and bedtime need to be consistent and predictable. Though this can be difficult for parents who have trouble structuring their own lives, it will benefit everyone in the family. Where there is an adequate schedule which includes some flexibility on special occasions and weekends, children learn to accept and expect their daily routine. They enjoy it. Where there is not an adequate daily routine, children fight every transition and can make meal times and bedtime a daily torture for the entire family.

Children who "won't" go to bed at night have discovered how to be more powerful than their parents. This kind of problem can be corrected with the investment of a week of instituting and enforcing an appropriate bedtime. To succeed parents must be prepared to stay firm with their intention and endure their child's rage and his attempts to manipulate them to forego the bedtime they have set.

Older school-aged children still need a schedule and routine they can depend upon. They need established study times for homework, limits on TV time, and time to play outdoors and with other children. Enforcing TV limits and study time require energy and commitment from parents. Their firm consistency teaches children to make and keep commitments to themselves and to respect themselves.

School-age children also need chores and responsibilities that are appropriate and possible for them to handle. Table setting, helping with dishes and clean up, emptying trash, and caring for their own rooms are tasks that teach necessary life skills. Ideally parents assign the child's chores and teach him to initiate the task on his own. For example, the trash has to be emptied by 5:00 P.M. each day. If the child forgets, he experiences a consequence of not doing his job. He might lose his TV time that evening. Parents provide consequences for not getting a job done rather than using their energy to remind the child repeatedly that he has a job to do. Parents who remind their children of everything are not allowing them to learn from the consequences of the choices they make. These parents don't like being a "bad guy" and taking a privilege away so they try to prevent the necessity for a consequence by remembering for their children.

Effective consequences for misbehavior and irresponsible behavior make the child's world smaller and limit his freedom. The goal is to teach him that freedom and responsible behavior go hand in hand. Consequences like staying in his room, losing TV or telephone privileges, restrictions on bicycles, and grounding confine the child, restrict his freedom, and teach him to face himself by limiting his ways of escaping from the results of his own choices. The child is responsible when he breaks a rule or ignores a responsibility. Parents are not guilty. Their job is to be reliable teachers who consistently enforce the house rules.

Being loving and firm are parental responsibilities, part of being grown-up parents. Parents who have not grown up themselves have trouble being responsible parents and are overindulgent and reluctant to require enough from their children. Parents need to tend to their own growth and let go of being children themselves in order to parent their children well.

When children break rules they are not "bad". They are exploring and testing to find out how their world works and where their limits are. If they experience consistent, reasonable consequences for misbehavior, they learn that responsible behavior is smart and helps them feel good about themselves. If they get away with misbehavior often enough, they learn that misbehavior works enough of the time to make it an acceptable risk.

If children get away with most of what they do at home, they will push for limits in the larger world outside the family. Misbehavior in school reflects a need for more structure at home as well as in the classroom. Teenagers who break the law are still trying to find where the limits are. Unfortunately, even our courts often give young people more chances rather than giving them a reasonable punishment that teaches them that limits do exist and that they too must respect those limits in order to live in society.

Brad was four years old when his father called me. Steve and his wife, Joan, were worried about their son. He was an extremely difficult child, and they were at their wit's end.

I met with Steve and Joan and Brad. Brad seemed to be a normal child, but he was somewhat anxious and constantly tried to involve one or the other of his parents in his play. They kept their attention focused on what Brad was doing so that it was difficult to talk with them with their child in the room.

Steve and Joan were both high achievers who pushed themselves beyond the limits of their available time and energy. They didn't understand why Brad was not as interested in being a good boy and pleasing them as they were in being good, high achieving parents.

Instead of setting limits with Brad and giving him consequences when he chose to break the rules, Steve and Joan talked to Brad. They tried to reason with him and persuade him to be good. They fussed over him in a worried way. They watched every bite of food he ate to be sure he was eating enough.

Brad was a bright little boy and had figured out just how to be powerful with his parents. He mirrored back to his parents rebellious parts of themselves that they feared. He refused to be a pleaser as both his Mother and Dad were locked into being. He wouldn't eat for them; he refused to be the good little boy they begged him to be. He got away with lots of rebellious behavior. He had them stumped and he knew how to frustrate them. He wasn't happy in the tense, busy environment they created for him. He reflected his parents' high level of stress and anxiety.

As Steve and Joan learned to set reasonable limits for themselves and created a more realistic structure for their family, they were more relaxed and calm. They also were learning to give Brad choices that respected his autonomy. Brad learned that if he cooperated in getting dressed before breakfast, he could have time to watch his favorite cartoon before leaving home for his pre-school. If he chose not to cooperate by putting on his clothes, he lost his cartoon time. He learned that he could choose how much and what he would eat from his plate at dinner. But he also learned that having dessert or a snack later depended upon his cooperating at meal time. If he refused to eat then, he didn't get to eat later.

Brad learned that "no" meant no and "yes" meant yes as Steve and Joan learned to be consistent with him. Brad relaxed and became a much happier child. And Steve and Joan were finally able to enjoy their son rather than fearing him and his behavior. As they were able to recognize and own the Pusher and Pleaser parts in themselves, they also claimed the Rebel in themselves. Brad no longer had to mirror the Rebel for them. Brad, Steve, and Joan were each free to be more whole, to relax, and enjoy life and each other. Steve and Joan no longer had to try to make Brad a perfect child or be perfect parents themselves. Now that they were able to appreciate and accept themselves without having to be perfect, their marriage improved. Little Brad no longer had to be in the middle, the focus of all their concerns, and their distraction from the challenge of becoming truly intimate with each other.

CHAPTER XXI

LIMIT SETTING VS. CONTROLLING

Isn't setting limits the same as trying to control other people? I hear this question frequently when I am teaching about limit setting.

Fear of limit setting mirrors fear of personal power. People who fear their own power tend to project or see that power in others, not in themselves. They feel powerless and are afraid others will be able to control them.

Control by other people is an illusion born of this pattern of disowning (or projecting) personal responsibility and power. We all possess free will. We choose what we manifest in our lives. When we see clearly that we are responsible for ourselves, we also realize that other people have the same power, choice, and responsibility for their lives. We do not control others anymore than they control us. When we know the power we have over our own choices, we also know the limits of the power we have over others or they over us.

As parents, we are responsible for providing a structure of moral, spiritual, emotional, and physical principles for our children to absorb. Young people will question these principles as they grow into adult maturity, but they need to encounter and absorb a parental structure in order to evolve their own standards as they become adults. In setting limits with children, our intention is not to control them. Our intention is to help them experience the consequences of the choices they make.

If a teenager is to be in from a date by 11:30 P.M., he chooses either to comply with that house rule or to disregard it. If his choice is to disregard the rule, he also is choosing the consequences of breaking that rule. He might be grounded for several days. The severity of his penalty will depend upon how late he is, whether or not he calls to explain his situation and the reason for his delay, and his previous record of responsible behavior.

He makes his own choice freely. The rule does not control him. It is designed to teach him and to offer him protection as he begins to move more and more freely in the larger world outside his family.

CHAPTER XXII

LIMIT SETTING WITH PARENTS

Limit setting is important, even with parents. Ideally as you grow to maturity and learn to nurture yourself successfully, you know how to find your center, and from that center, you are able to define the boundaries that separate you from others. You accept your individuality and your personal responsibility for your life. You know how to say no to yourself and to your peers. Saying no to your parents without feeling guilty is another challenge to be faced.

Both parents and children may long to hold on to the past and cling to the dependency that existed between them during the children's younger years. But the normal task for maturing young adults is claiming responsibility for their own lives. Inevitably there are conflicts and clashes with parents as this maturing occurs.

For many years I remained in a childlike posture with my parents. I tried to keep them happy rather than finding the courage to risk being my real self with them. I was afraid to upset them by doing or saying anything that might bring their anger, disapproval, or disagreement. I relied on physical distance between my home and theirs to assure that my life was separate from theirs.

I was 35 when I was forced to face the issue of separating my life from theirs. Both of them became invalids, and I moved them to the city where I live so I could supervise their care. I had to balance their needs and their distress about their helplessness with my needs and the needs of my family. This was no small task. It is difficult to move from a child-parent relationship to an adult-adult relationship which still honors the original parent-child experience. I had not yet accomplished that transition and now there was the further challenge of becoming parent for my parents who now were more helpless than children.

While I was struggling with this dilemma, my teenage daughter was busy setting limits with me, insisting that she be respected as a competent young adult and trusted to behave responsibly. One day, after a particularly challenging confrontation with her, I realized that she certainly was not protecting me from her growing up. Why was I still protecting my parents from the reality that I was no longer just their daughter but also had a full life of my own with major adult responsibilities? With my daughter as my teacher, I began a similar process of separating my life from theirs while still being sensitive to their needs and feelings and responsible for their care.

Young adults need to learn to say no in a loving way to parental demands that are not appropriate. I should have done so much earlier in my life. My life and my relationship with my parents would have been much happier. But I avoided that challenge because I was afraid to claim my responsibilities to myself as an adult and afraid to grow up and let go of the familiar feeling of security that I associated with not upsetting my parents. I let the Saboteur that discounted my needs and feelings stay in charge of my life.

Breaking away is a challenge that adult children may avoid for years. The Saboteur loves to use guilt and fear to convince them that they simply can't be honest with their parents. Both generations cooperate in pretending to defy the passage of time and changing life circumstances. Such deception is costly to everyone involved. It sabotages everyone and keeps all the players stuck in a developmental stage they long since outgrew chronologically. Their growth, development, creativity, and sense of mastery of life's challenges are stunted.

It is a joy to realize how parents improve and enjoy life more as their adult children decide to grow up, relate to them differently, and set limits with them. Daughters are teachers for mothers. Sons are guides for their fathers. Everyone is better after the initial "change-back" reaction to the young adult whose behavior challenges the accepted norm for family members. Inevitably the family exerts pressure on the person who is the change agent in an attempt to get him to reassume his old role so other family members will not have to make changes, too. If he withstands this assault, the family will readjust to a new balance and everyone will grow in the process. Family life will be more enjoyable for everyone when the readjustment is completed.

Again, Gibran in *The Prophet* beautifully expresses the necessity for space between generations. "Your children are not your children. They are the sons and daughters of Life's longing for itself. They come through you but not from you, and though they are with you yet they belong not to you . . . You may house their bodies but not their souls . . . You may strive to be like them, but seek not to make them like you."

Angela was 35 years old and lived with her younger sister. Neither of them had married and neither of them held jobs. They lived on trust funds provided for them from their family's substantial investments.

Angela was terribly unhappy and was plagued by depression and illness. Her younger sister seemed more content, but actually she was terribly dependent on Angela. Angela's parents depended on her, too. Because they traveled extensively, she was expected to manage their property and their business while they were away.

When Angela came into therapy, she was desperate for help.

She felt terrible physically. She was unhappy without a job, but she hadn't been able to get one, despite having an excellent education and a good mind. The problem was that Angela still looked like a child and, an awkward child at that. She had little sense of herself and no self-confidence. Prospective employers were put off by her appearance and her difficulty in making contact with other people. But Angela knew she wanted to grow. She was determined to solve her problems.

Working with Angela was exciting. She was willing to do whatever it took to take charge of her own life and create herself the way she wanted to be.

Gradually she realized that separating her life from her sister's and her parents' was crucial for her development. As long as she invested her time in taking care of their needs when they could have done so themselves, she was ignoring her own needs and her goals for herself. She decided that continuing in her current life pattern was not in her best interest.

As she made plans to find a house of her own, separate from her sister, and at some distance from her parents, the rest of her family became quite upset. How could Angela do such a selfish, thoughtless thing? Wasn't she grateful for all her parents had done for her? Wasn't she ashamed to even consider such a rash move? Angela's sister was distressed, too. Who would do her errands, pay her bills, clean her house for her if Angela moved out. She couldn't let her do that to her!

During this period Angela received lots of support and understanding from other people in her therapy group. With their encouragement, she was able to set limits with her parents and her sister and make her own personal declaration of independence. Once she separated her life from theirs, she moved toward a new career that she wanted and away from the professions her parents had encouraged her to pursue. As Angela made these changes, a new, attractive, even confident young woman began to emerge. She felt fine physically now. She cared how she looked. She loved her new home. She was excited with her new career and confident that she would be good doing what she had always secretly dreamed of doing. She was ready to try out dating and looked forward to creating a new family of her own.

Angela's parents and her sister benefited, too. Once they saw that their old hold on Angela no longer existed, they had to make changes. Angela's sister learned to live independently; eventually she decided to claim the full extent of her own life and resources. Angela's parents took over their business and managed their own affairs. They also prospered. With Angela as an example, everyone discovered more of his strength and resources. And as they began to use these resources, they found themselves to be happy.

Previously this family had lived as if children were children forever; as if children existed to serve their parents. They pretended time stood still and continued to relate to each other as parents and children even though the children were adults entering the middle years of their lives.

Facing reality and realizing that Angela was going to claim her own life opened the door for everyone else to grow, too. The best part is that everyone enjoys life more and appreciates and respects each other in a completely new way. There's no longer any reason to pretend that life and families never change and grow.

CHAPTER XXIII

THE LOVING ART

Limit setting is a loving art, essential to nurturing yourself successfully. It helps you create the structure your relationships require, so you avoid the trap of loving others too much while neglecting your responsibilities to yourself. Limit setting faces you with the responsibility you hold for the quality and meaning of your life. It frees you from the mire of ill-defined, consuming relationships that drain your energy and deplete your resources. Limit setting creates choices.

Choices allow flexibility, offer opportunities, and open the doors that lead to creative successful living. Choices generate power and energy for living. They challenge you to explore, to grow, and to transform. The choices you make are the crux of your life.

Choices occur continuously, whether you notice yourself making them or not. Choices are your responsibility whether you are aware of them or not. Your choices make you the person you are. No one else is responsible.

It's your choice moment by moment:

1. To keep yourself centered in the energy of love or to allow fear to throw you off balance.

2. To respect your power and responsibility for your own life and claim the fullness of your potential,

including the talents and resources you possess.

3. To create a better world by expressing the talents you possess and taking constructive action to solve problems, enhance the beauty and quality of life, and create new choices.

4. To communicate your ideas and share what you're learning through networks of friends and business associates, community organizations, the arts, writing, radio, and television.

5. To enjoy fully each moment you live and to embrace the goals you set as you release yourself into positive action directed by your higher dimensions of consciousness.

6. To reap the most learning and growth from the experiences of your life.

7. To face the question of death of the physical body so you can fully embrace the joy and responsibility of living.

8. To attune yourself to your higher dimensions of consciousness in order to experience the peace and harmony of that space and to avail yourself of the wisdom and guidance available to you from the higher reaches of your being.

Centering yourself in the energy of love you are open to these choices for creativity, growth, and contribution to your world. You are able to distinguish what is your responsibility from what belongs to another. No longer trying to love others too much, you are free to enjoy relationships defined by adequate boundaries that allow each person the fullness of his being within a context of love, acceptance, sharing, and intimacy. Through centering, you choose to allow love to direct you rather than giving fear the power it seeks to sabotage your life.

Remember that courage is the other side of fear. Where your fears run deep, you have evidence of the strength of the courage you also possess. Centering yourself in love transforms your perspective so you can see the personal courage your fears reflect. After all, it is your courage that has kept you going all the years of your life in the face of your fears. Love and courage have directed you and truly are stronger than your fears and your Saboteur. The fact that you are alive today is proof of that! You are winning and your winning will be easier and easier as you see yourself more and more clearly and lovingly and transform your Saboteur into the courageous ally you deserve.

CHAPTER XXIV

STOPPING SELF-SABOTAGE

Stopping the Saboteur is a moment-by-moment process. When you see your Saboteur clearly and recognize its efforts to sabotage you with negative, fearful thinking, you can say no to it, refuse to energize its crippling suggestions, and transform your thinking into a powerful positive force in your life.

It is also helpful to be aware of patterns of self-sabotaging behavior that occur when you fail to gain control of the Saboteur at the mental level of your functioning. When the Saboteur controls your thinking, some of these patterns may emerge in your behavior.

1. Self-sabotage is happening when you deny your responsibility for your life and try to attain your goals by establishing and maintaining symbiotic relationships with others. You are afraid you don't have the resources you need to be successful on your own. You look to others to "help" you. You sabotage yourself by trying to manipulate others to do your bidding so you can avoid taking responsibility for the work, resources, and effort required to reach your goals. You love others too much and neglect truly loving and nurturing yourself.
2. Self-sabotage is operating when you ignore your own limits and set yourself up for financial, physical, emo-

tional, and mental exhaustion. You are a helper, often ignoring your own needs and interests. You consistently end up appearing to be someone else's victim.

3. Self-sabotage happens when you neglect limits and boundaries within yourself and between yourself and other people. No matter how positive your mental attitude, the discipline of respect for the boundaries between people is a critical factor for success. Self-saboteurs presume on their relationships with others who eventually become angry and retaliate.
4. Self-sabotage is happening with people who talk as if they are masters of positive thinking yet are not successful financially or emotionally. The pattern at work here is one of predicting and expecting great success while neglecting to take into account unconscious negative input from the Internal Saboteur and the reality limits of time, available resources, and necessary hard work. Unless these factors are taken into account, no amount of positive thinking can prevent an eventual disaster from occurring.
5. Self-saboteurs make financial decisions based on the success they expect before that success is a reality. In the process they overextend themselves, and put enormous pressure on themselves to make miracles happen so they can support their inflated expenditures and commitments.
6. Self-saboteurs experience periods of despondency and depression that are a marked contrast to their periods of positive thinking. Usually they are unwilling to deal with the issues that lie beneath the surface of their lives.
7. Self-saboteurs often are extremely bright people who have almost always been able to talk their way out of any situation. As children, they were easily able to manipulate their parents with their quick wit and ease with words. Consequently, no one set appropriate

limits for them when they were growing up. They have no experience of limits and consequences, and operate as if their day of reckoning will never come. When it does, they are surprised and angry. And they usually feel that the problem was caused by someone else. They defend themselves by blaming others.

8. Self-saboteurs are trying to take care of other people whose love they desire, but feel unworthy of having. They lead these people to expect more from them than they can provide, and then overextend themselves so as not to disappoint them.
9. Self-saboteurs do not feel adequate to win playing by the rules. They like the excitement of big stakes and set up situations that require too much of themselves or of others. Their fear is that they could not succeed in rational, responsible, business projects. So they push for whatever is risky and exciting. In the process they may have some amazing successes, but their destructive, unworthy side will arrange eventually to destroy what they have attained.
10. Self-saboteurs have great difficulty letting go. They cling to the past, to destructive relationships, to ideas and strategies that do not work. They have trouble completing what they start and often have lots of unfinished projects that they juggle. They look busy but accomplish little.

Let's contrast these patterns of sabotaging behavior with behavior patterns that are evident in the lives of people who are successful, attain their goals, and enjoy their lives.

1. Successful people think positively, accept limits and boundaries, and practice healthy self-discipline and the discipline of respect for boundaries between people. They are able to attain the substantial, real, lasting success that eludes others. They do not presume on their relationships with others. They establish healthy

contracts with other people and keep their end of the bargain.

2. They make financial decisions that are sound, recognizing the necessity for dealing with the reality of the present while planning for and expecting greater success in the future. They do not get ahead of themselves financially.
3. They maintain an even disposition which flows from a strong connection with spiritual dimensions of consciousness. They tune in to the world around them and are sensitive to the responses they receive from other people. They are skilled communicators. They make adjustments to changing circumstances and remain flexible enough to respond effectively to shifts in the economy and the community in which they work.
4. They are able to take full advantage of their brightness and intelligence because they have learned to harness these resources and make them work for, rather than against, them. They take into account the costs of the choices they make and are prepared to deal with the consequences of those choices.
5. They do not waste their time and energy imagining that they are the victim of someone else's actions or mistakes. They are clear in their thinking and aware of the choices they are making moment by moment.
6. They feel worthy themselves and adequate to face the challenges life presents. They recognize that others are also worthy and adequate to take full responsibility for their lives as well. They do not attempt dramatic rescues of others; nor do they foster emotional or financial dependence. They encourage others to be self-sufficient and successful, also.
7. They see the value of structure, and respect the rules that apply in business and interpersonal contracts. They find excitement and fulfillment in accomplishing

their goals and in taking each step toward the realization of those goals. They do not look for excitement in breaking the rules and trying to beat the system. They know that success requires personal commitment, self-discipline, and productive activity and risk taking.

8. Because they respect limits and boundaries, they are able to achieve success that is unlimited. By respecting limits and keeping boundaries, they master the Internal Saboteur and transform his energy into a positive power in their lives. They free themselves to realize their full potential for success and happiness. They are open to experience the abundance life offers and the pleasure that comes with using their resources and abilities to the full extent of their powers.

You can accomplish miracles when you accept the value and essential importance of yourself, other people, and the context within which you meet and interact. Virginia Satir calls this the target position in communication and relationship with others. Winners know that everyone counts and is important in any system, be it a family, business, government or religious system. Losers ignore either themselves, others, or the context in which they operate. In that process, they sabotage their success, and confirm their loser position.

The Saboteur tells you that you don't count and ignores your needs, feelings, and goals. It discounts others, too, and expects defeat and disappointment for everyone. It is the agent of fear.

Stopping self-sabotage by facing, mastering, and transforming the Saboteur frees you to accept and honor the whole of who you are. You stop discounting others, too, and relate to them in love and with respect. You keep your boundaries intact and say yes and no honestly and without fear. Success and prosperity embrace you. You are a master of the loving art.

CHAPTER XXV

BEYOND YOUR BOUNDARIES

Once you learn to value and maintain boundaries that embrace you and give you form, definition, and structure, you are ready to move into new realms of pleasure, success, and prosperity. You are ready to plunge into the fullness of living, knowing you will not be lost or destroyed in the process.

When you master your boundaries, you feel safe with yourself, safe enough to step out into the world and take full responsibility for the strengths and resources you possess. As you feel your boundaries intact, firm and strong, you know you are free from undue dependence on others. You know you can establish and maintain healthy, productive relationships with others. You no longer cling to the past. You are strong enough to resist encroachments on your space, time, resources, and interests from parasitic people who seek to feed themselves on your life resources. You are able to fend for yourself, provide for your own needs, and give yourself adequate protection.

Beyond your boundaries lies the universe with all its incredible beauty, richness, and abundance. Appreciating this abundance is taking the time to really look at the stars and galaxies, at our oceans and the life that inhabits them, at the leaves on a tree, the petals of a flower, snow flakes in winter, the blades of grass that carpet your lawn. Can you imagine how many individual drops of water join to form a lake or how many individual cells are contained within the universe of one human body?

Within your boundaries and beyond, there is incredible abundance when you allow yourself to see it. Once you recognize this abundance and allow yourself to experience it fully, you can claim your share of it. To do so, you must reach out and give unstintingly of your talents and abilities and open yourself to receive a plentiful supply of whatever you need in return.

Experiencing abundance means being able to both give and receive without reservation. One is the complement of the other. There is no way to experience one without the other even though you may not see that connection. There is no way to inhale without exhaling, too. There is no way to live outside the universal flow of giving and receiving, creating and allowing.

When you open your eyes and realize who and what you really are, you see that you are part and parcel of the whole of the universe. Whether you call this whole God, or Universal Good, or Divine Energy, you are a part of It. Just as each petal is a vital part of the beauty of the flower it helps form, each human being is a tiny part in the whole body of God's universe.

Just as God creates, you, as a part of God, create also. You create the reality you experience. Through the powerful instrument of your mind, you conceive, imagine, and manifest what your thoughts direct you to create.

If you allow the Saboteur to fill your mind with fear, you create the very painful, awful situations you dread. If your mind is filled with love, you create peace, health, happiness, and abundance.

There is no middle ground. You either plant your feet firmly in fear, or you surround yourself in the energy of love. You may shift rapidly from one dimension to the other as moment-by-moment you choose the reality you experience.

When you choose love, you are totally immersed in its warmth and soothing energy. When you choose self-sabotaging fear, it vibrates within you, consuming your attention and setting off negative reactions throughout your physical body.

The important thing is to learn to recognize when the Saboteur has you in its grip. As soon as you know what is happening, you can say no to the Saboteur, deepen your breathing and release your fears with every exhalation. You can remind yourself to recenter in the energy of love and shield and ground yourself in this love.

You are not a helpless victim of a fate directed by external forces. You are author of the reality you create.

Look at the reality you are spending your life creating. Are you directing a self-destructive, self-sabotaging drama, ignoring your boundaries and the boundaries between yourself and others? Or are you secure within your boundaries and respectful of the boundaries that separate you from others? Are you allowing your creativity and wisdom to guide you toward an intention and purpose you have set for your life?

Purposes and goals are essential to successful living. These purposes evolve and change over the years, but are always necessary if you are to feel worthy, and find meaning in your life. A sense of your purpose enables you to survive through difficult and troublesome times. Your purpose can be great or small. The size of the task is less important than the necessity that a direction and goal exist.

Moving toward that goal is a process that fuels itself continually as you take one step after another. Each single step counts, even though the final outcome may not yet be apparent. Each single step is crucial to the success of the larger goal, even though the present step may seem to fail or be less than you hoped. It is a teacher if you are willing to look at it and see what its lesson is.

Patience is your ally as you face the challenge of discovering what lies along the path you seek to follow. As you wend your way deeper and deeper into that territory, you may feel as if you are moving into a void where you have no idea what you will encounter. You only know that each step requires your utmost strength and mental concentration. You are living on the edge, fully embracing your creativity and trusting your wisdom to guide you.

The challenge is to free yourself from enslavement of any kind and open yourself to the inner wisdom and guidance that are available when you tune into higher dimensions of consciousness. With your boundaries about you like a warm coat in winter, giving you comfort and protection from external forces, you are ready to move into the full realization of your potential for love, happiness, prosperity, service, success, and fulfilling relationships.

With your boundaries intact, you can take your place in this world, fulfill your purposes and goals, and be a healthy, functioning part of the whole of the universe you help comprise. Like a healthy cell in a healthy body, we are healthy individuals in a world that will become healthy, too.

The health and well-being of our planet, our country, our state, our city, and our neighborhood community reflect the physical, emotional, mental and spiritual health and well-being of each individual that inhabits them. By being fully who we are as separate individuals, we move beyond our boundaries into new realms of joy and creativity in relationships that in turn energize, affect, and bring healing to the larger world we share.

Life is like a tree laden with golden coins. Do we fear the tree and avoid seeing its beauty and richness? Do we walk by on the other side of the street, afraid to come too close to such a magnificent sight? Or do we dare embrace the tree, climb its branches, shake its limbs, and reap its harvest of bounty and love?

It's my choice. It's your choice. And at every moment

we choose again; the game of fear and self-sabotage, clinging to the past, or growing up and living in love. Which are you choosing now? What will you choose next? The power and the choice are yours. The outcome is yours to reap. Loving choices are for successful people! You deserve abundance, prosperity, happiness, and health. Will you claim what is yours for the taking?

CHAPTER XXVI

TRANSFORMING THE SABOTEUR

As I completed this book last January, my Saboteur was busy doing its best to slow me down, discourage me, and suggest that I was out of my mind to think I'd ever be successful as a writer. In my mind, I heard comments like;

"No one will enjoy reading this. It isn't good enough."

"Who do you think you are to imagine you have anything worthwhile to say?"

"Your examples aren't very interesting. You should have used dialogues."

"This can't compare with your favorite books. You just don't have what it takes to write interesting material."

"Let's don't work on this now. You really need to be doing something else."

"You think you're smart with all this stuff about a Saboteur. I'm lots smarter than you are. You'll never outwit me. See I'm still around and I'm powerful."

When I recognized my heavy-handed Saboteur doing its thing once more, I realized yet another time how tempting it was for me to pay attention to its comments. I activitated my nurturing self, laughed at the Saboteur while appreciating its persistence and creativity, and finished my work. After sending the manuscript out to potential publishers, I put it aside and released it completely.

Since then I have written a regular newspaper column and have begun a second book. I've become lots more comfortable with myself as a writer. I have continued my weekly radio program and continued to work with the principles described in this book.

When the response I wanted from a good publisher finally came, I took my manuscript out of its place in my desk and opened myself to it once again. And I did yet another rewrite. But this time, I know this book is valuable and I trust myself more deeply than I ever have before. When I came to this final chapter and read the comments I had heard from my Saboteur just nine months ago, I was delighted to realize just how foreign those negative, fearful, discouraging words are to me now.

For my Saboteur has begun to join forces with me. It respects my authority over my life now and knows that its fearmongering foolishness is rarely powerful with me anymore. It certainly hasn't gone away, but it wastes lots less energy trying to undermine me. Consequently, I have more energy and creativity available for doing what I truly want to do. I've come a long ways toward taming the monster and it's becoming quite an ally.

Thanks for joining me in reading this book. I feel close to you and have enjoyed creating this for you. Good luck with your challenges. Your life is your very own magnificent creation. Be the artist you are!

BIBLIOGRAPHY

THE PHYSICAL DIMENSION

THE INDIVIDUAL

Barbach, Lonnie, Ph. D. *For Each Other, Sharing Sexual Intimacy*. Garden City, NY: Anchor Books/Doubleday, 1983.

Barbach, Lonnie Garfield. *For Yourself, the Fulfillment of Female Sexuality*. New York: Anchor Books/Doubleday, 1976.

Gach, Michael Reed with Carolyn Marco. *Acu-Yoga, Designed to Relieve Stress and Tension*. Tokyo: Japan Publications, Inc., 1981.

Hay, Louise L. *You Can Heal Your Life*. Farmingdale, NY: Coleman Publishing, 1984.

Hittleman, Richard. *Richard Hittleman's Yoga: 28-Day Exercise Plan*. New York: Bantam Books, 1973.

Ponder, Catherine. *The Dynamic Laws of Healing*. Marina del Rey, CA: DeVorss & Company, 1972.

Ponder, Catherine. *The Healing Secrets of the Ages*. Marina del Rey, CA: DeVorss & Company, 1967.

Siegel, Bernie S., M.D. *Love, Medicine & Miracles*. New York: Harper & Row, 1986.

Simonton, O. Carl, M.D., Stephanie Matthews-Simonton, and James Creighton. *Getting Well Again*. Los Angeles: J. P.Tarcher, 1978.

FAMILIES AND RELATIONSHIPS

Cameron-Bandler, Leslie. *Solutions, Practical and Effective Antidotes for Sexual and Relationship Problems.* San Rafael, CA: FuturePace, Inc., 1985.

Lillibridge, E. Michael, Ph.D. *The Love Book for Couples Building A Healthy Relationship.* Atlanta, GA: Humanics Ltd., 1984.

McClendon, Ruth and Leslie B. Kadis. *Chocolate Pudding and Other Approaches to Intensive Multiple-Family Therapy.* Palo Alto, CA: Science and Behavior Books, Inc., 1983.

Satir, Virginia. *Conjoint Family Therapy.* Palo Alto, CA: Science and Behavior Books, Inc. 1967.

Satir, Virginia. *Making Contact.* Millbrae, CA: Celestial Arts, 1976.

Satir, Virginia. *Peoplemaking.* Palo Alto, CA: Science and Behavior Books, Inc., 1983.

THE WORLD WE SHARE

Ferguson, Marilyn. *The Aquarian Conspiracy.* Los Angeles: J. P. Tarcher, Inc., 1980.

Naisbitt, John. *Megatrends.* New York: Warner Books, 1982.

THE EMOTIONAL DIMENSION

Bass, Ellen and Louise Thornton. *I Never Told Anyone, Writings by Women Survivors of Child Sexual Abuse.* New York: Harper & Row, 1983.

Bolen, Jean Sninoda, M.D. *Goddesses In Everywoman.* San Francisco: Harper & Row, Inc., 1984.

Brandon, Nathaniel. *The Psychology of Romantic Love.* Los Angeles: J. P. Tarcher, Inc., 1980.

Branden, Nathaniel. *The Psychology of Self-Esteem,* New York: Bantam Books, 1969.

Butler, Sandra. *Conspiracy of Silence: The Trauma of Incest.* San Francisco: Volcano Press, 1980.

Cowan, Connell and Melvyn Kinder. *Smart Women, Foolish Choices.* New York: Crown, 1985.

Forward, Dr. Susan and Joan Torres. *Men Who Hate Women & The Women Who Love Them.* Toronto: Bantam Books, 1986.

Friday, Nancy. *My Mother My Self.* New York: Delacorte Press, 1977.

Haley, Jay. *Uncommon Therapy, The Psychiatric Techniques of Milton H. Erickson, M.D.* New York: W. W. Norton, 1973.

Herman, Judith Lewis. *Father-Daughter Incest.* Cambridge, MA: Harvard University Press, 1981.

Leonard, Linda Schierse. *On The Way To The Wedding, Transforming the Love Relationship.* Boston: Shambhala, 1986.

Leonard, Linda Schierse. *The Wounded Woman, Healing the Father-Daughter Relationship.* Athens, OH: Swallow Press, 1982.

Lerner, Harriet Goldhor, Ph.D. *The Dance of Anger, A Woman's Guide to Changing the Patterns of Intimate Relationships.* New York: Harper & Row, 1985.

Norword, Robin. *Women Who Love Too Much.* Los Angeles: J. P. Tarcher, Inc., 1985.

Shainess, Natalie, M.D. *Sweet Suffering, Woman As Victim.* Indianapolis: The Bobbs-Merrill Co., Inc., 1984.

Woodman, Marion. *Addiction to Perfection.* Toronto: Inner City Books, 1982.

GESTALT THERAPY

Fagan, Joen and Irma Lee Shepherd. *Gestalt Therapy Now.* New York: Harper Colophon Books, Harper & Row, 1970.

Latner, Joel, Ph.D. *The Gestalt Therapy Book.* New York: The Julian Press, Inc., 1973.

Perls, Frederick S., M.D., Ph.D. *Gestalt Therapy Verbatim.* Lafayette, CA: Real People Press, 1969.

Perls, Frederick S., M.D., Ph.D. *In and Out the Garbage Pail.* Lafayette, CA: Real People Press, 1969.

Polster, Erving and Miriam Polster. *Gestalt Therapy Integrated.* New York: Brunner/Mazel, 1973.

Rosenblatt, Daniel. *Opening Doors, What Happens In Gestalt Therapy.* New York: Harper & Row, 1975.

Stevens, John O., (ed). *Gestalt Is.* Moab, UT: Real People Press, 1975.

Zinker, Joseph. *Creative Process In Gestalt Therapy.* New York: Vintage Books, 1978.

TRANSACTIONAL ANALYSIS

Berne, Eric. *Beyond Games And Scripts*. New York: Grove Press, Inc., 1976.

Berne, Eric, M.D. *Transactional Analysis In Psychotherapy*. New York: Grove Press, Inc., 1961.

Berne, Eric, M.D. *What Do You Say After You Say Hello?* New York: Grove Press, Inc., 1972.

Goulding, Mary McClure and Robert L. Goulding. *Changing Lives Through Redecision Therapy*. New York: Brunner/Mazel, 1979.

James, Muriel. *Breaking Free, Self-Reparenting For A New Life*. Reading, MA: Addison-Wesley, 1981.

James, Muriel and Dorothy Jongeward. *Born to Win*. Reading, MA: Addison-Wesley, 1981.

Schiff, Jacqui. *Cathexis Reader, Transactional Analysis, Treatment of Psychosis*. New York: Harper & Row, Inc., 1975.

Steiner, Claude, Ph.D. *Games Alcoholics Play: The Analysis of Life Scripts*. New York: Grove Press, 1971.

THE MENTAL DIMENSION

PROSPERITY CONSCIOUSNESS

Cole-Whittaker, Terry. *How To Have More In A Have-Not World*. New York: Fawcett Crest, 1983.

Laut, Phil. *Money Is My Friend*. Hollywood, CA: Trinity Publications, 1978.

Leonard, Jim and Phil Laut. *Rebirthing: The Science of Enjoying All of Your Life.* Hollywood, CA: Trinity Publications, 1983.

Maltz, Maxwell, M.D., F.I.C.S. *Psycho-Cybernetics.* New York: Simon & Schuster, 1960.

Mandel, Bob. *Open Heart Therapy.* Berkeley, CA: Celestial Arts, 1984.

Orr, Leonard and Sondra Ray. *Rebirthing In The New Age.* Berkeley, CA: Celestial Arts, 1977 and 1983.

Patent, Arnold M. *You Can Have It All.* Piermont, New York: Money Mastery Publishing, 1984.

Ponder, Catherine. *The Dynamic Laws of Prosperity.* Marina del Rey, CA: DeVorss & Company, 1962.

Ponder, Catherine. *The Prospering Power of Love.* Marina del Rey, CA: DeVorss & Company, 1966.

Ray, Sondra. *Celebration of Breath.* Berkeley, CA: Celestial Arts, 1983.

Ray, Sondra. *I Deserve Love.* Millbrae, CA: Les Femmes, 1976.

Ray, Sondra. *Loving Relationships.* Berkeley, CA: Celestial Arts, 1980.

Ray, Sondra. *The Only Diet There Is.* Berkeley, CA: Celestial Arts, 1981.

Ross, Ruth, Ph.D. *Prospering Woman.* Mill Valley, CA: Whatever Publishing, Inc., 1982.

Sher, Barbara with Annie Gottlieb. *Wishcraft, How To Get What You Really Want.* New York: Ballantine Books, 1979.

Waitley, Denis. *10 Seeds of Greatness.* Old Tappan, NJ: Fleming H. Revell Company, 1983.

THE SPIRITUAL DIMENSION

Adler, Vera Stanley. *From The Mundane To The Magnificent.* York Beach, ME: Samuel Weiser, Inc., 1979.

Adler, Vera Stanley. *The Finding Of The Third Eye.* New York: Samuel Weiser, Inc., 1983.

Assagioli, Roberto, M.D. *Psychosynthesis.* New York: Penguin Books, 1965.

Capra, Fritjof. *The Tao of Physics.* Toronto: Bantam Books, 1976.

Easwaran. Eknath. *Dialogue With Death.* Nilgiri Press, 1981.

Fankhauser, Jerry, M.S.W. *From A Chicken To An Eagle.* Farmingdale, NY: Coleman Graphics, 1980.

Faraday, Dr. Ann. *Dream Power.* Berkeley, CA: Berkeley Publishing Corporation, 1972.

Faraday, Ann. *The Dream Game.* New York: Harper & Row, 1974.

Garfield, Patricia L., Ph.D. *Creative Dreaming.* New York: Ballantine Books, 1974.

Jampolsky, Gerald G. *Goodbye To Guilt, Releasing Fear Through Forgiveness.* Toronto: Bantam Books, 1985.

Jampolsky, Gerald G. *Love Is Letting Go Of Fear.* Berkeley, CA: Celestial Arts, 1979.

Jampolsky, Gerald G. *Teach Only Love, The Seven Principles of Attitudinal Healing.* Toronto: Bantam Books, 1983. 1983.

Joy, W. Brugh, M.D. *Joy's Way, A Map For The Transformational Journey.* Los Angeles: J. P. Tarcher, 1979.

McDonald, Phoebe. *Dreams, Night Language of the Soul.* Baton Rouge: Mosaic Books, 1985.

Moss, Richard, M.D. *The I That Is We.* Millbrae, CA: Celestial Arts, 1981.

Nelson, Ruby. *The Door Of Everything.* Marina del Rey, CA: DeVorss & Company, 1963.

Probstein, Bobbie. *Return To Center.* Marina del Ray, CA: DeVorss & Company, 1985.

Rodegast, Pat and Judith Stanton. *Emmanuel's Book.* New York: Some Friends of Emmanuel, 1985.

Small, Jacquelyn. *Transformers, The Therapists of the Future.* Marina del Rey, CA: DeVorss & Company, 1982.

Stone, Hal, Ph.D. *Embracing Heaven and Earth, A Personal Odessey.* Marina del Rey, CA: DeVorss & Company, 1985.

Stone, Hal, Ph.D. and Sidra Winkelman, Ph.D. *Embracing Our Selves.* Marina del Rey, CA: Devorss & Company, 1985.

Vaughn, Frances. *The Inward Arc.* Boston: Shambhala, 1986.